DELIGHTFUL DESIGNS
ADULT COLOURING BOOK

Animals, Flowers, Mandalas & Other Patterns

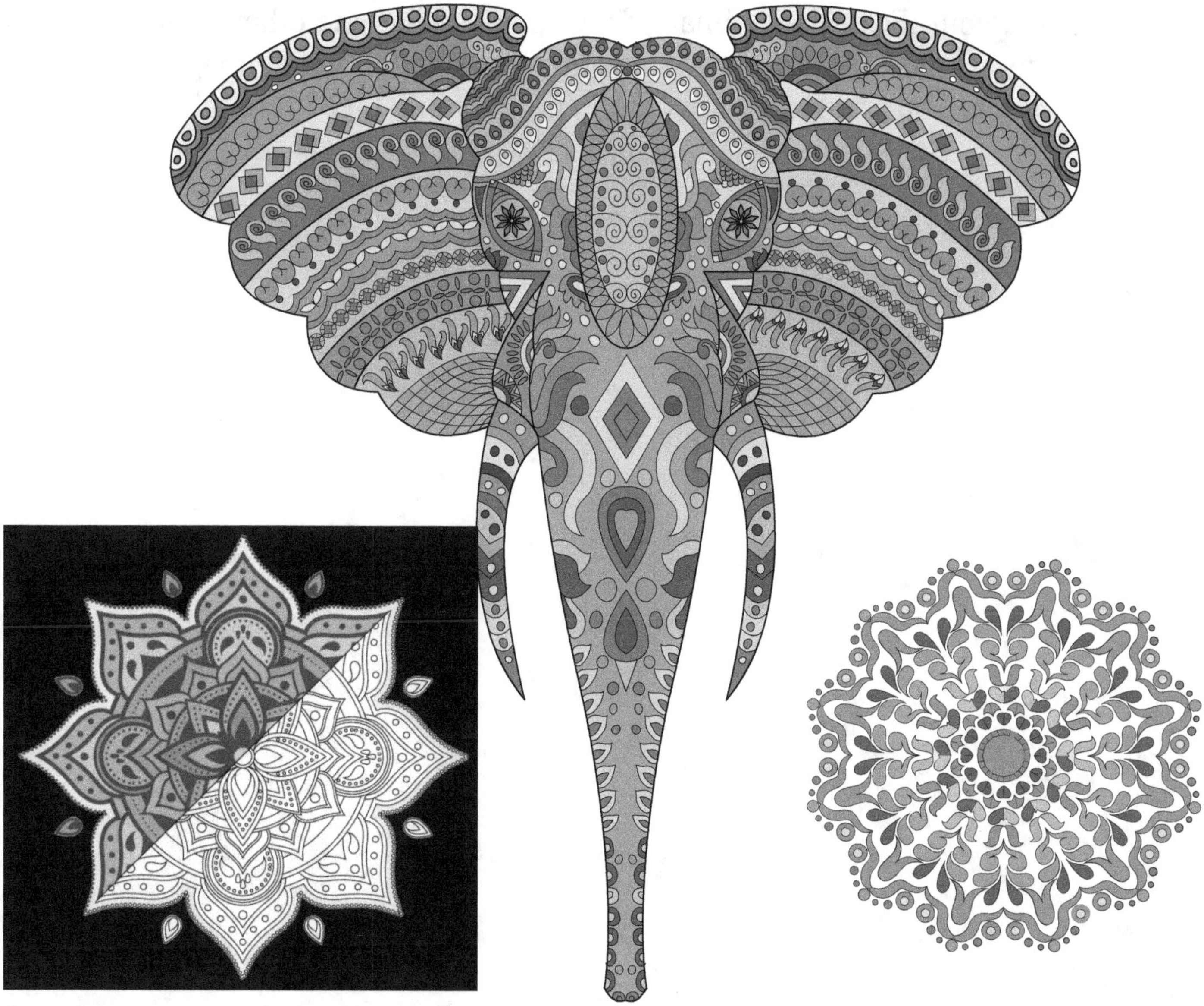

Paul Andrew Smith

©Paul Andrew Smith 2020 All rights reserved.

Relax and unwind with this amazing collection of intricate designs for you to colour. Featuring animals, flowers, mandalas and other beautiful patterns to use your creativity and artistic talent on. Each image is printed on one sheet of paper to allow for any bleed through.
Enjoy!

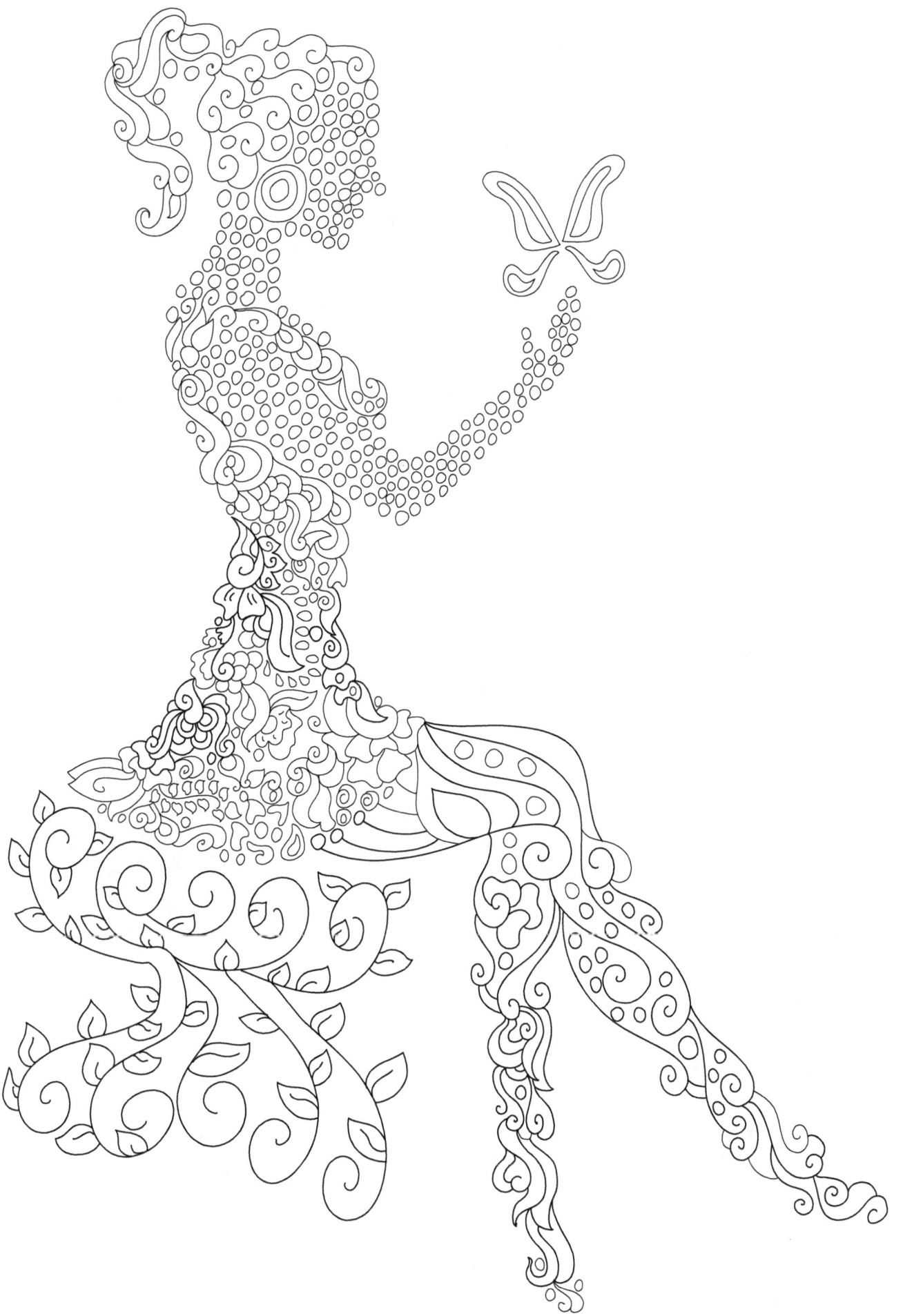

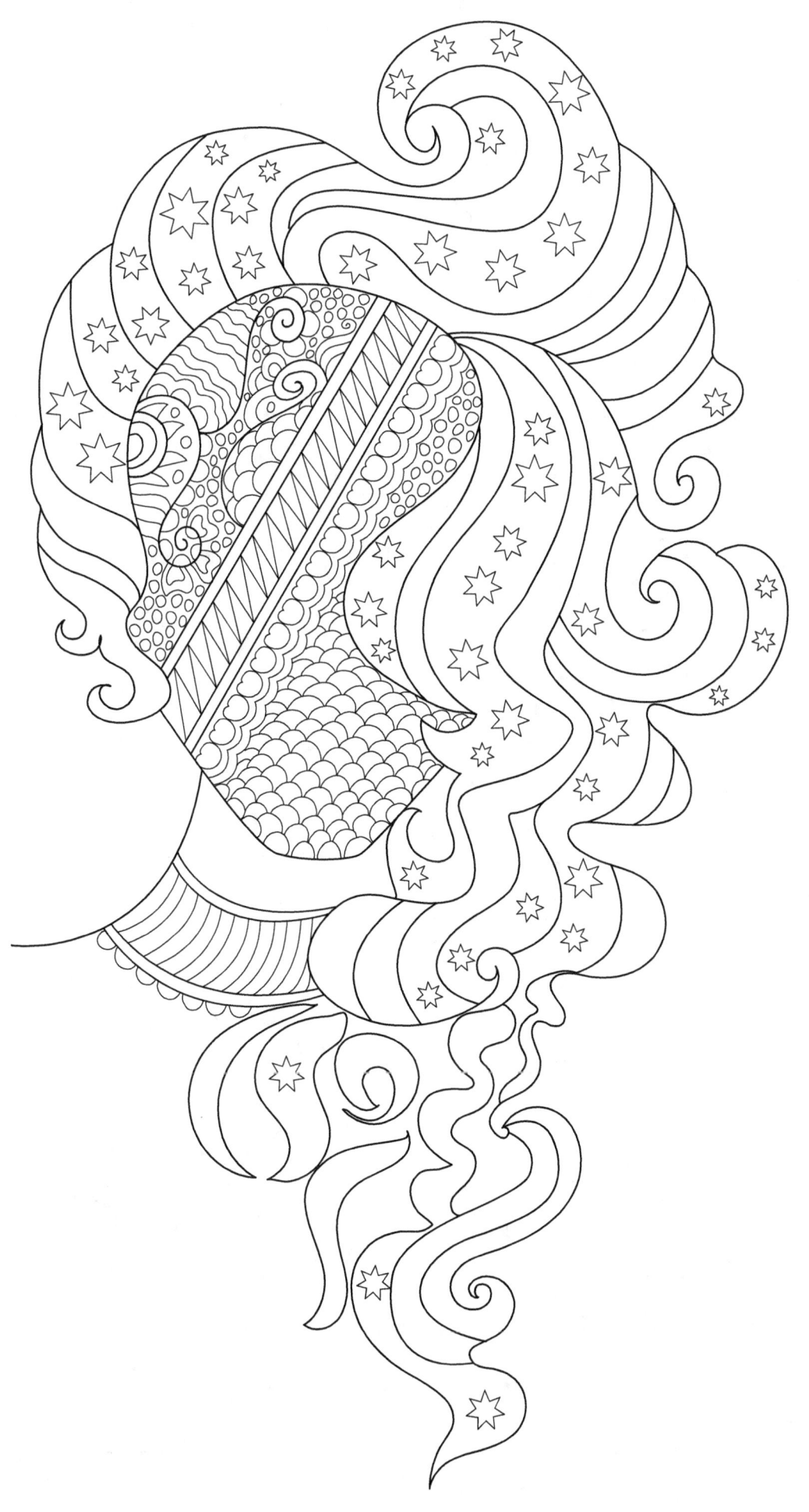

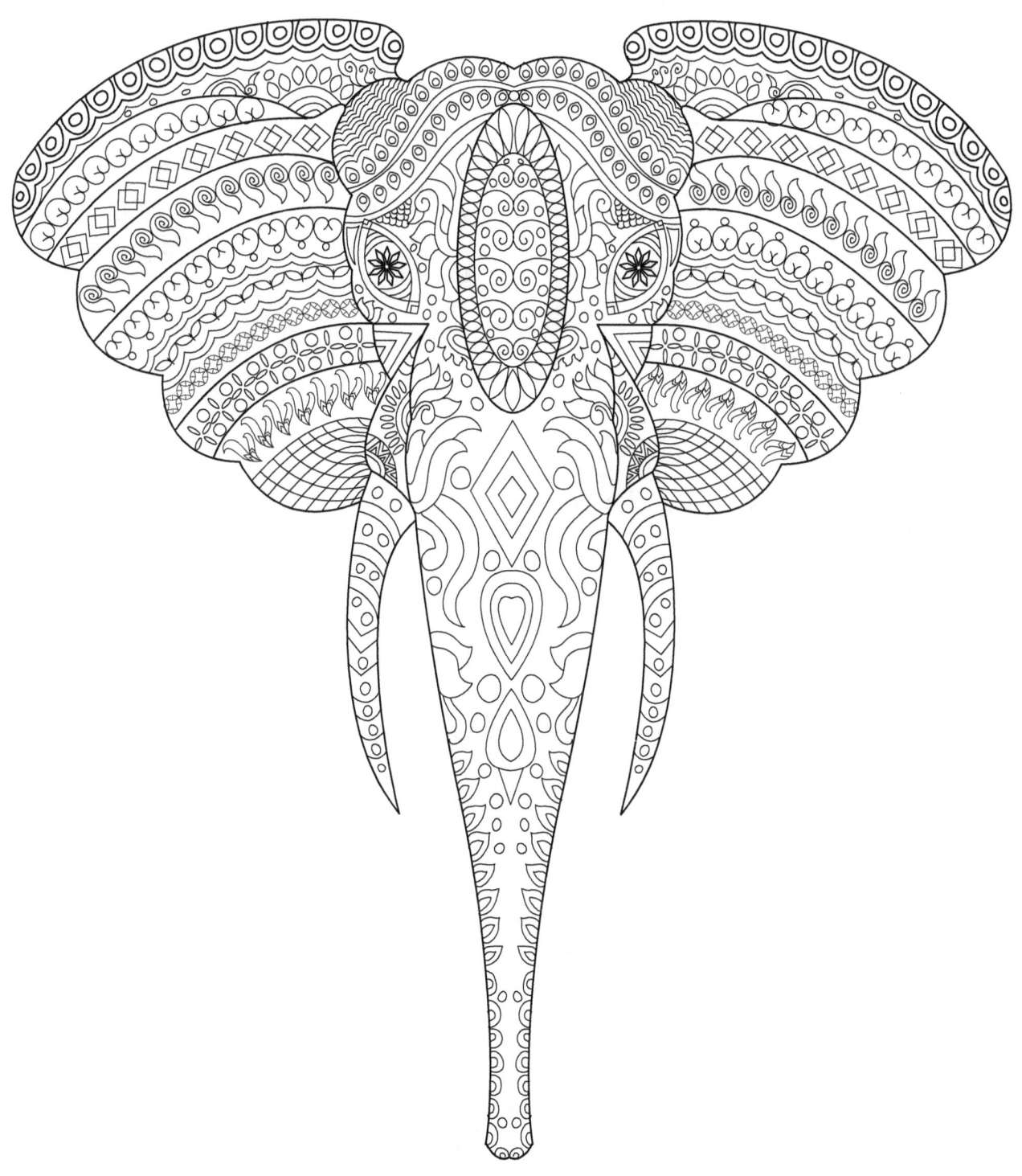

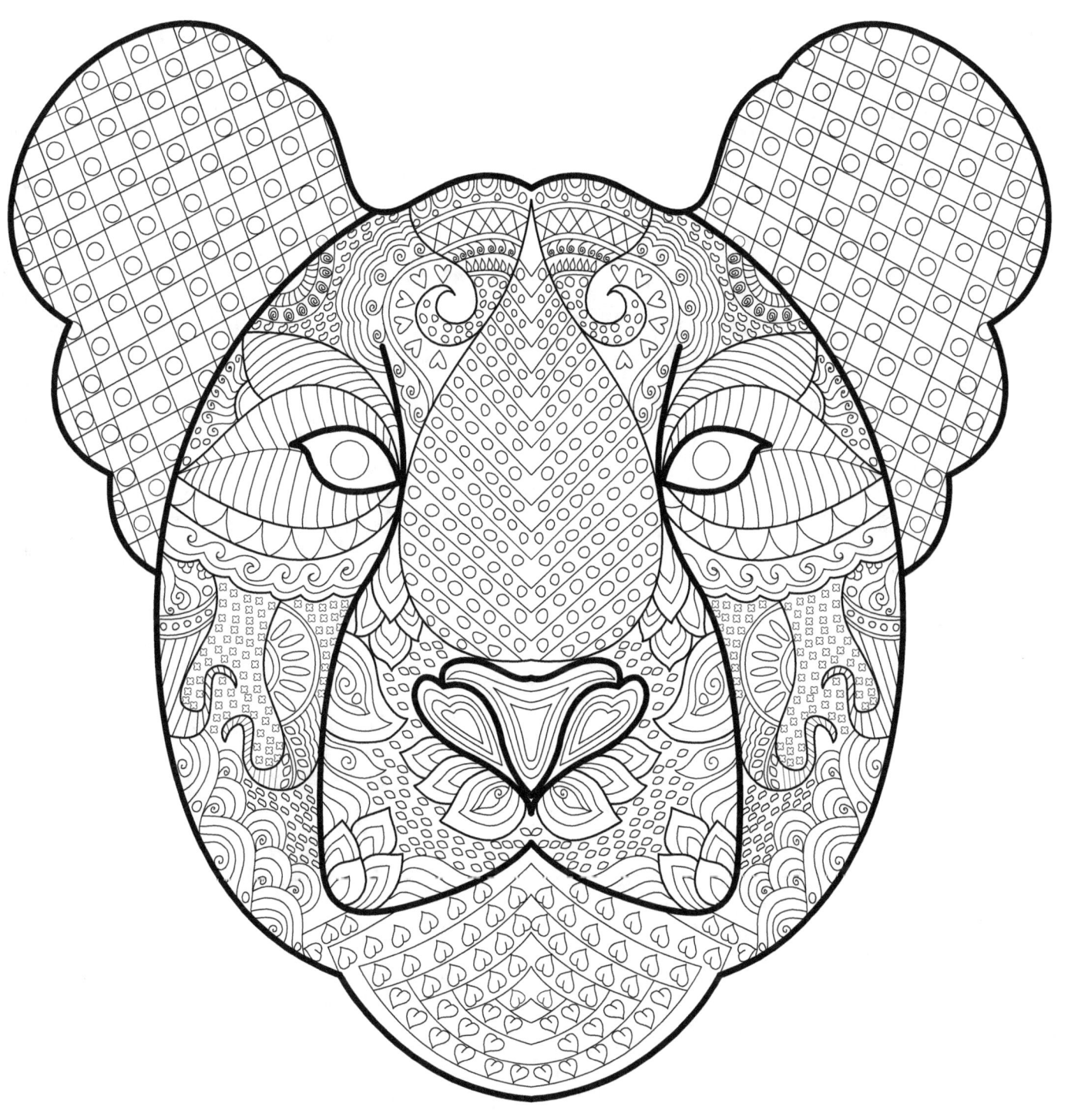

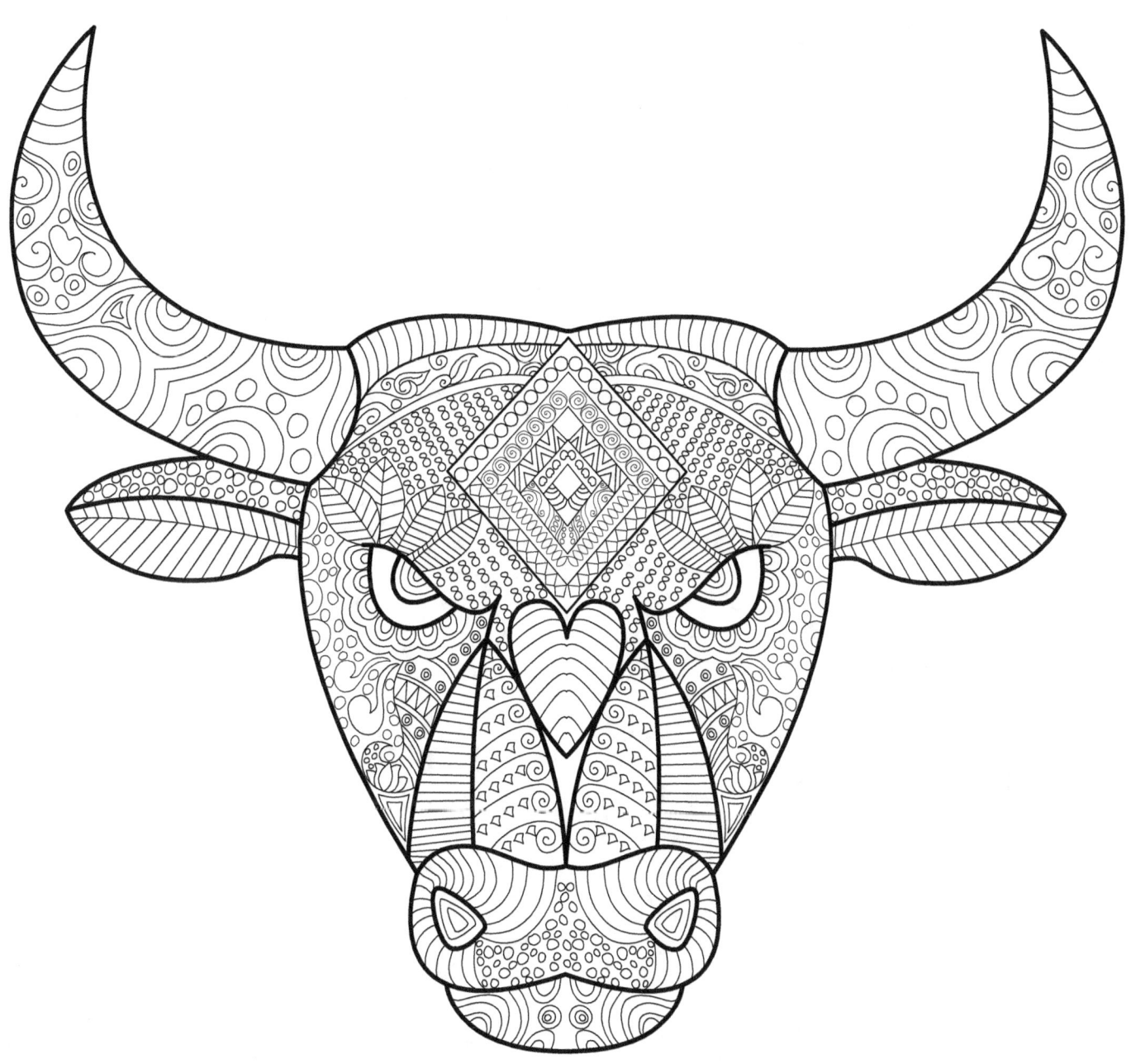

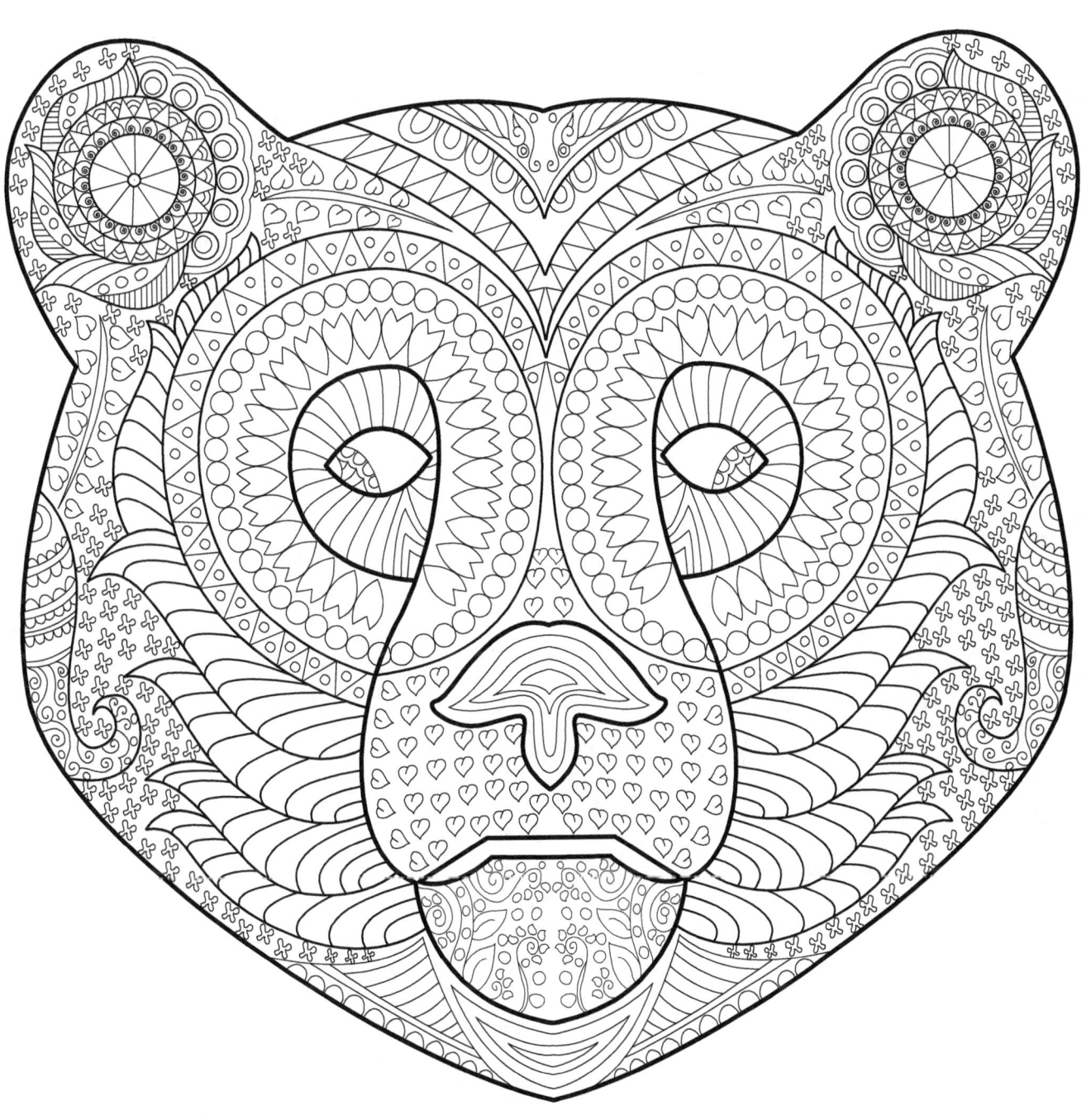

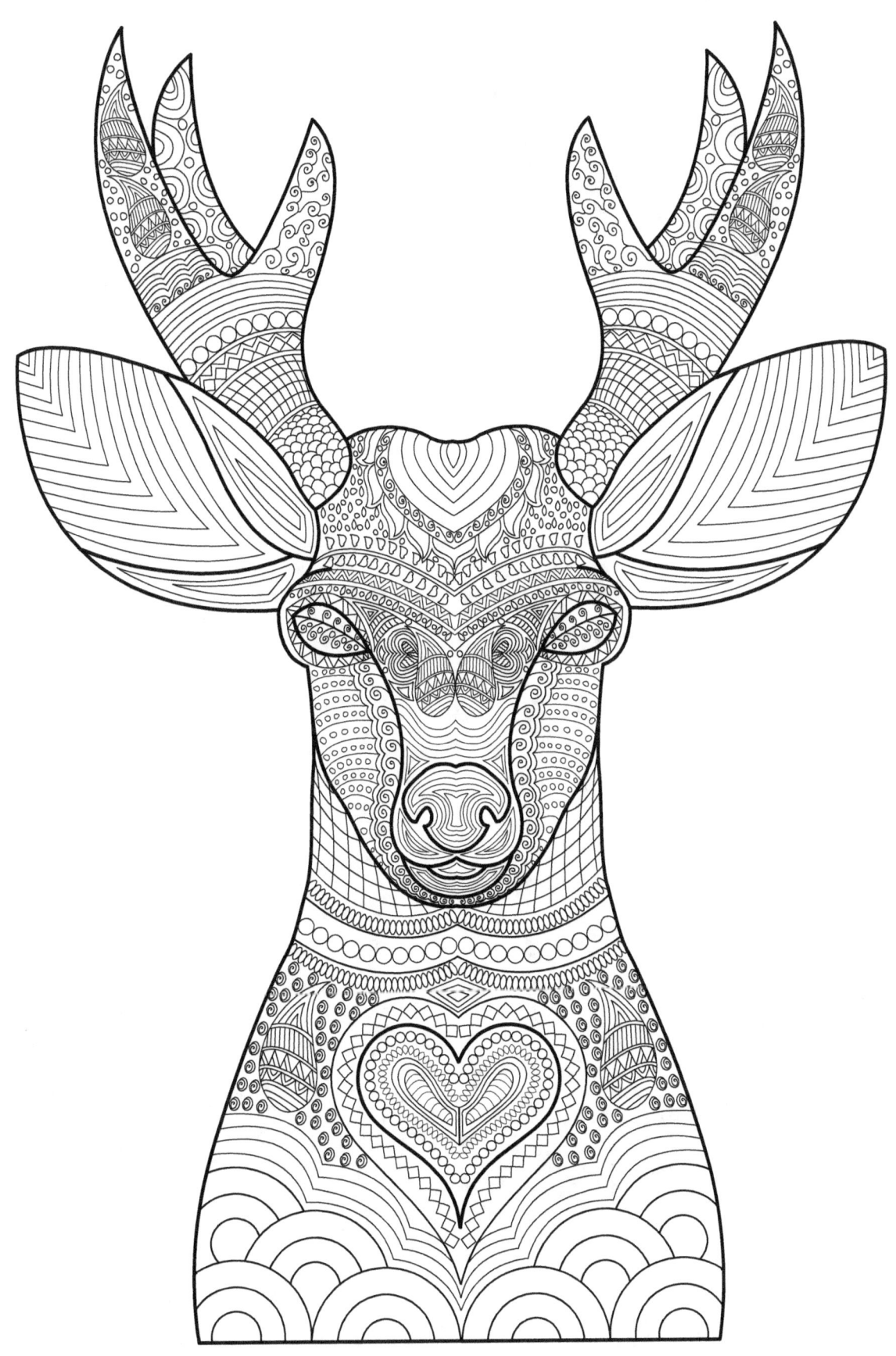

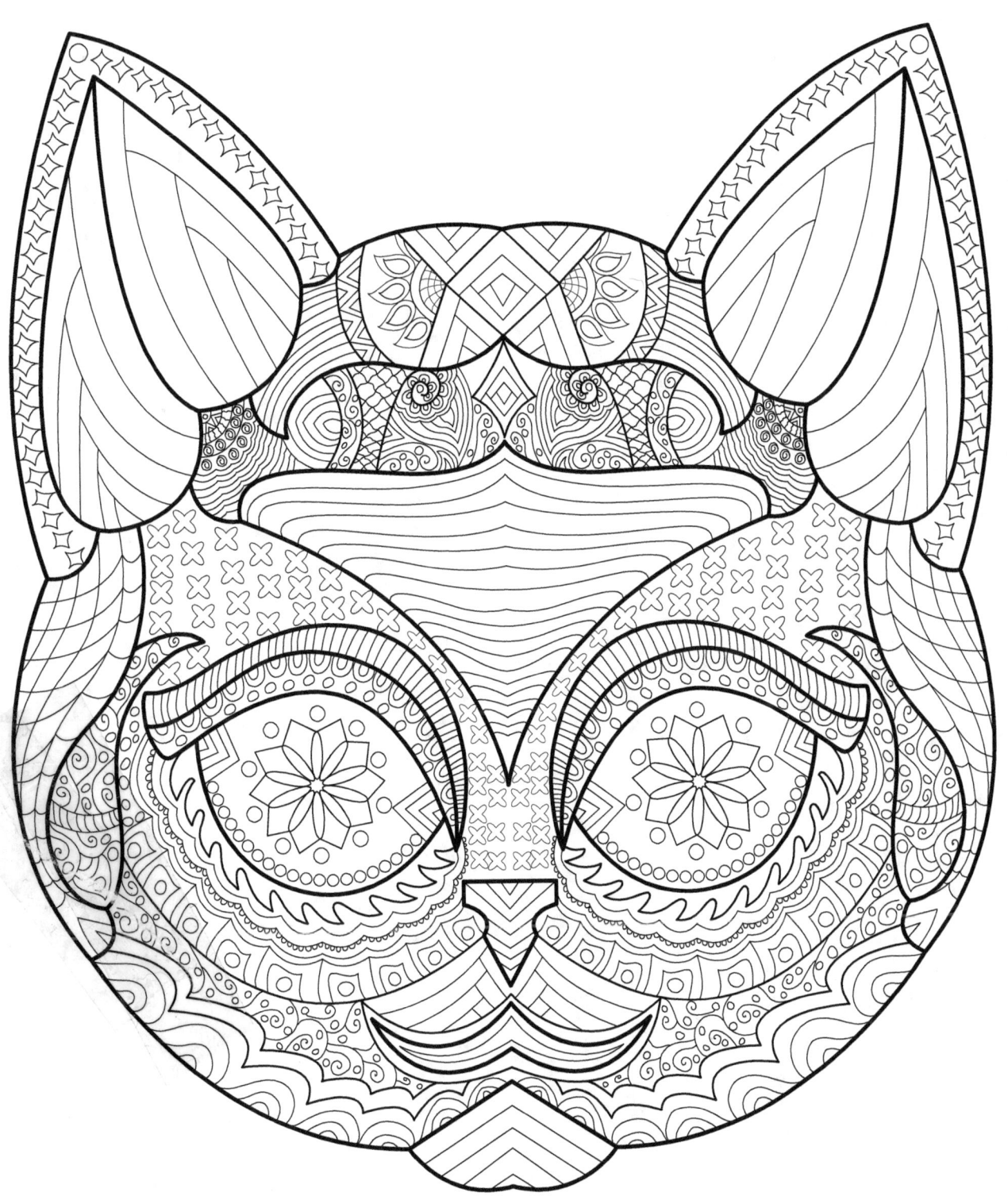

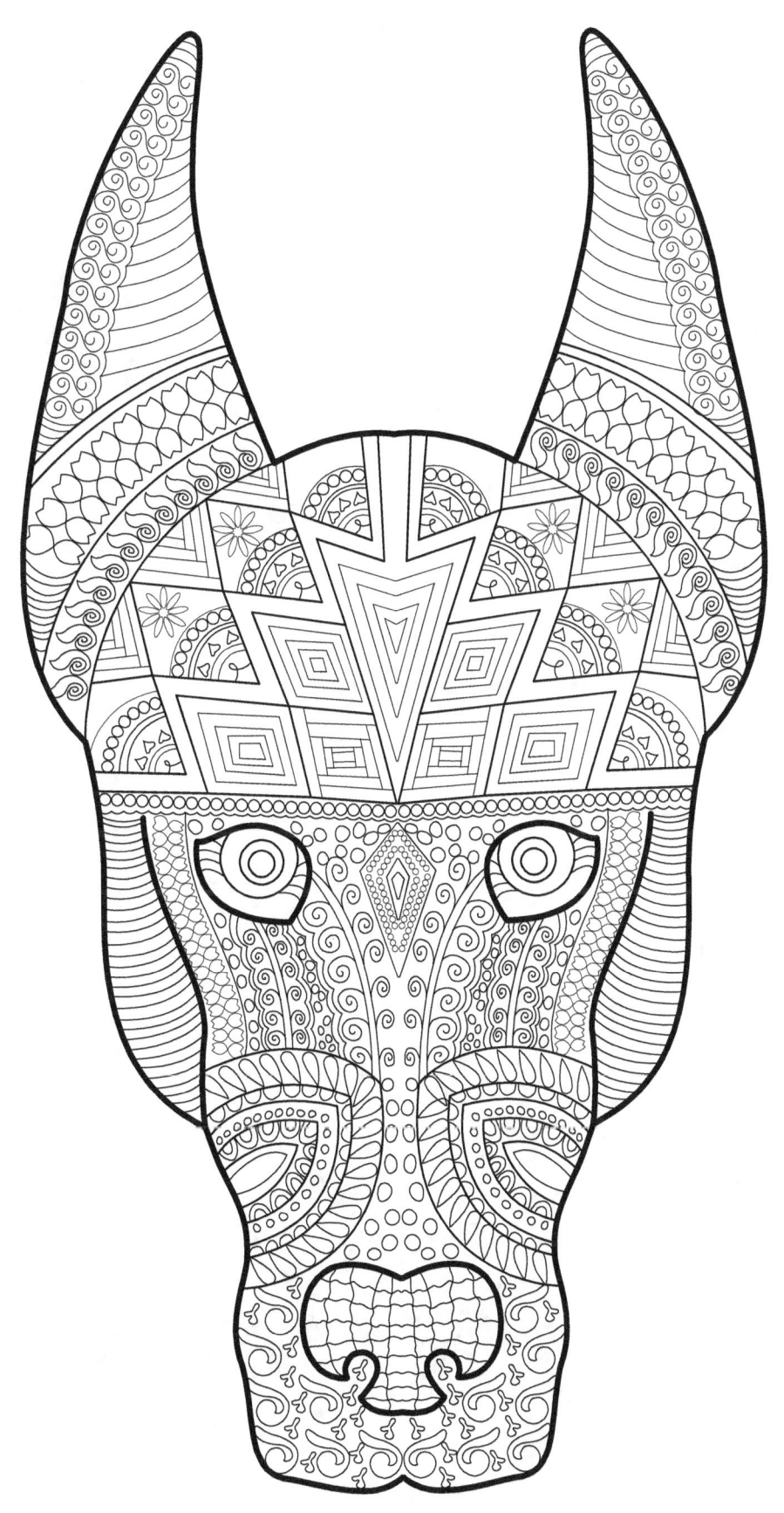

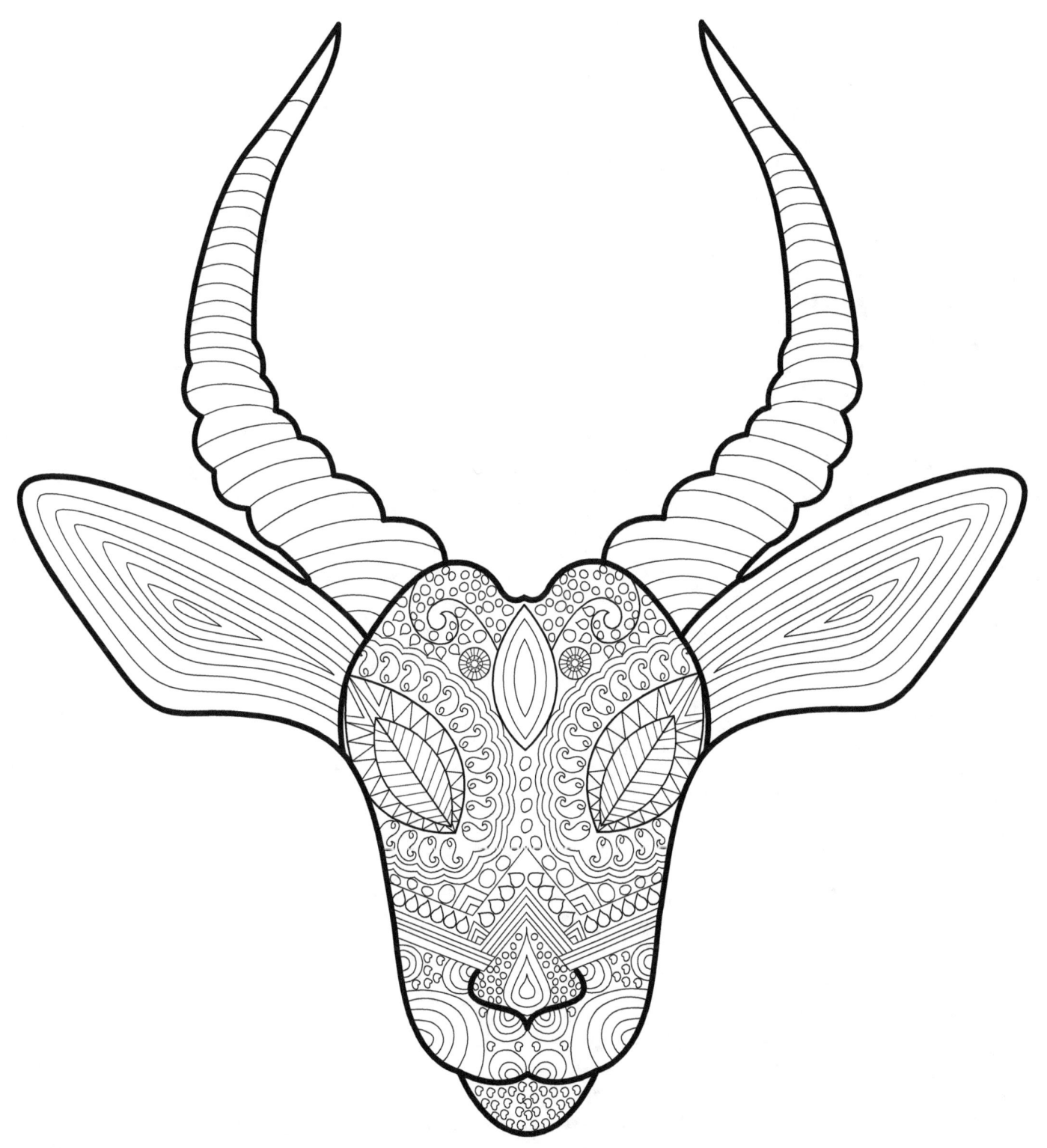

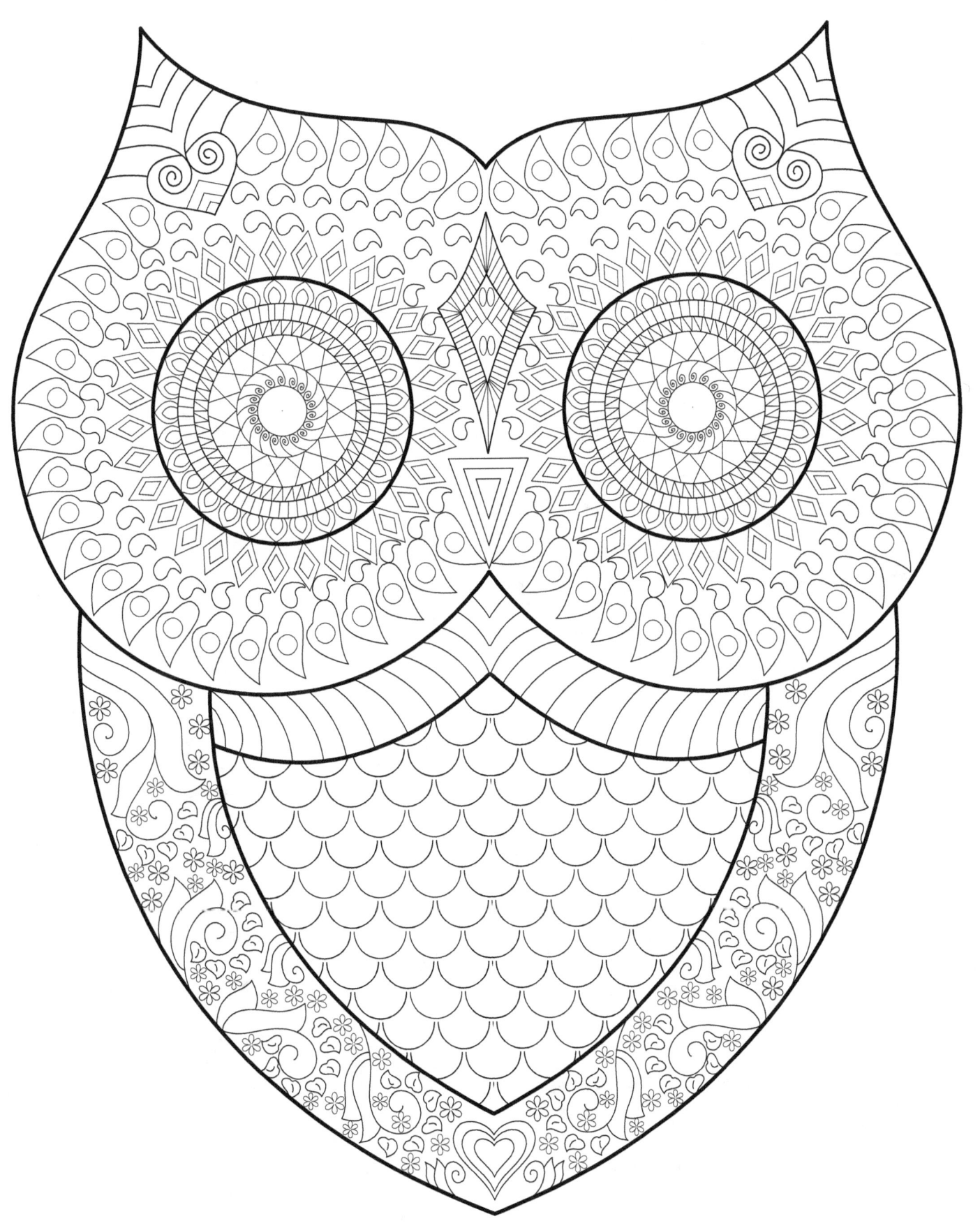

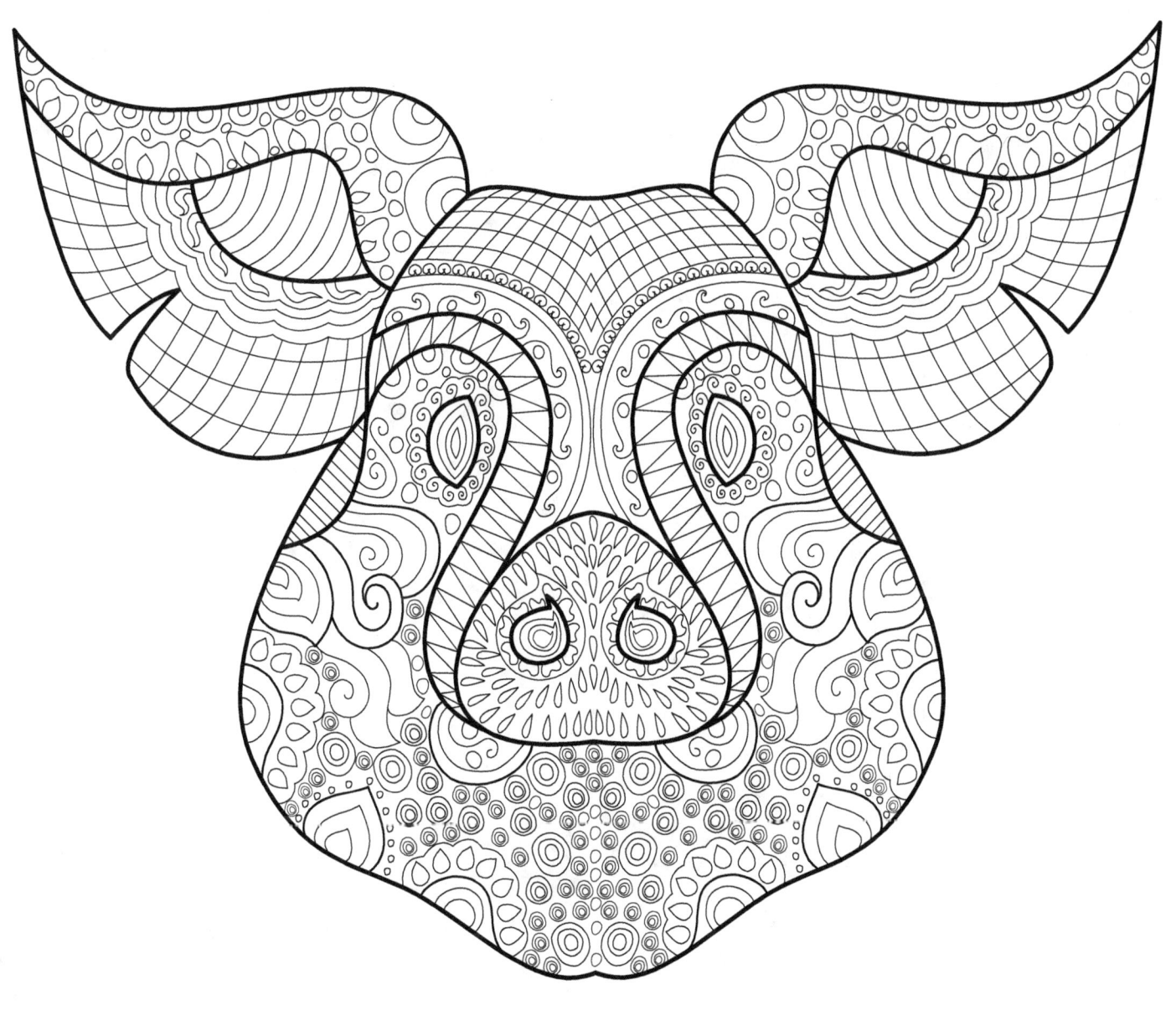

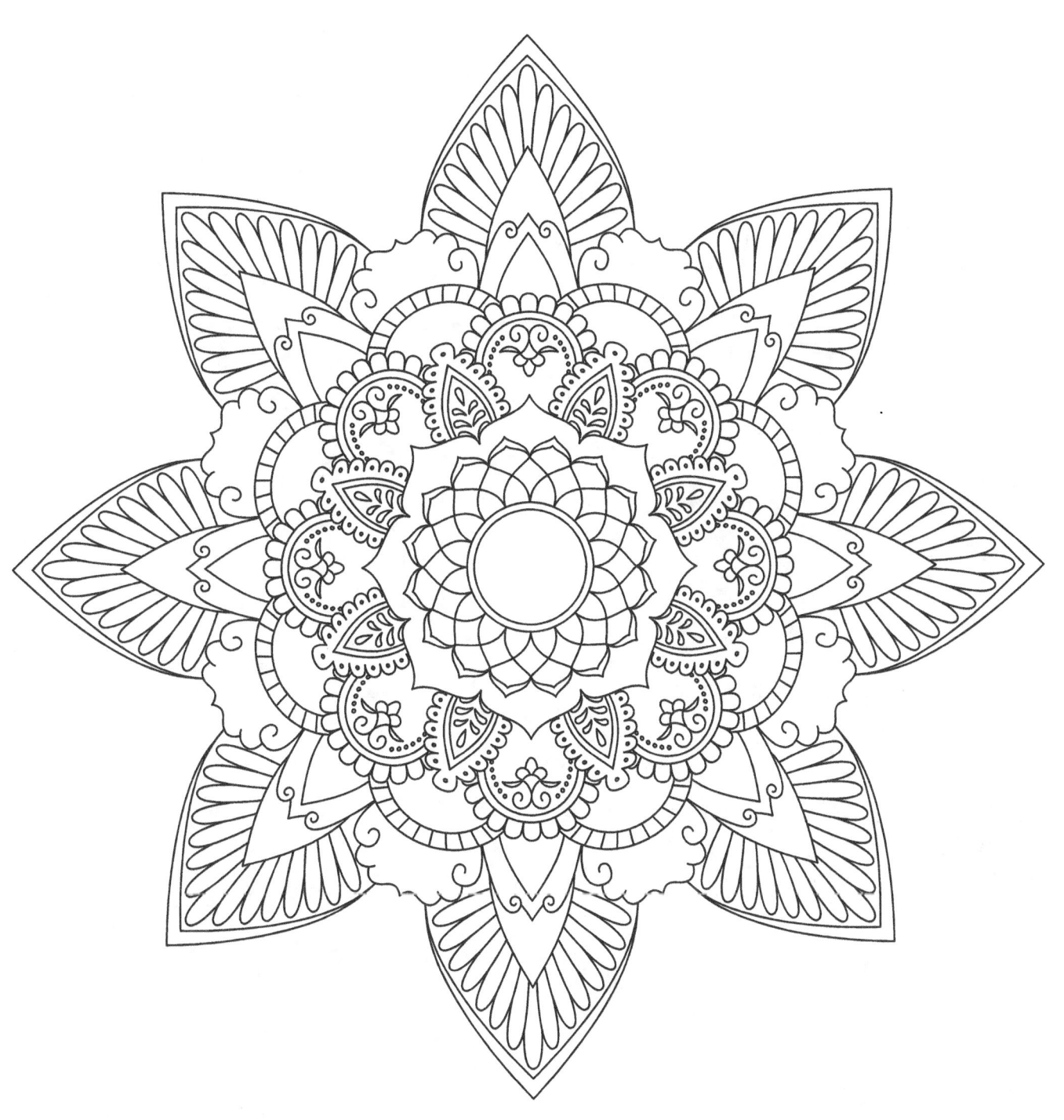

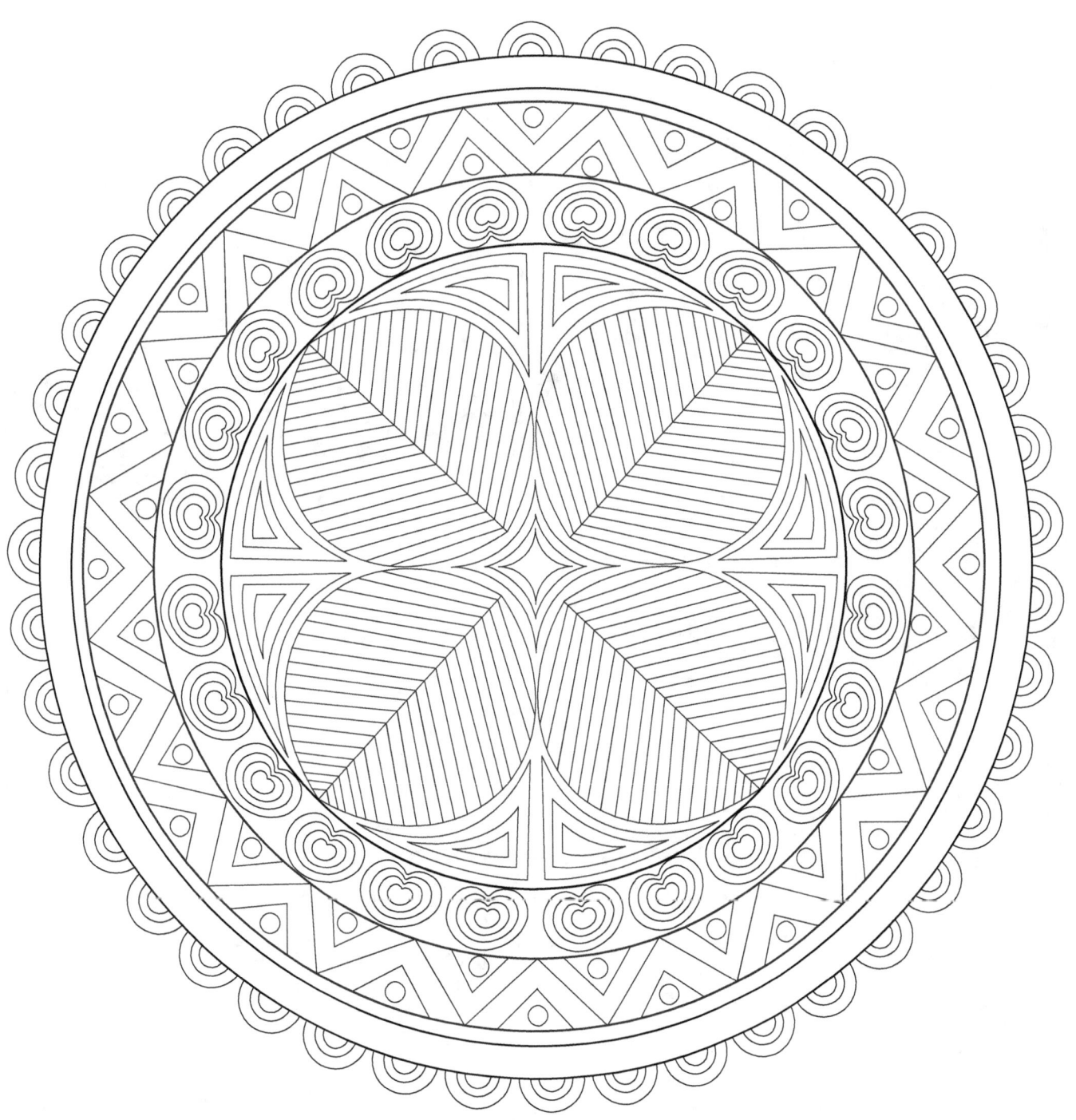

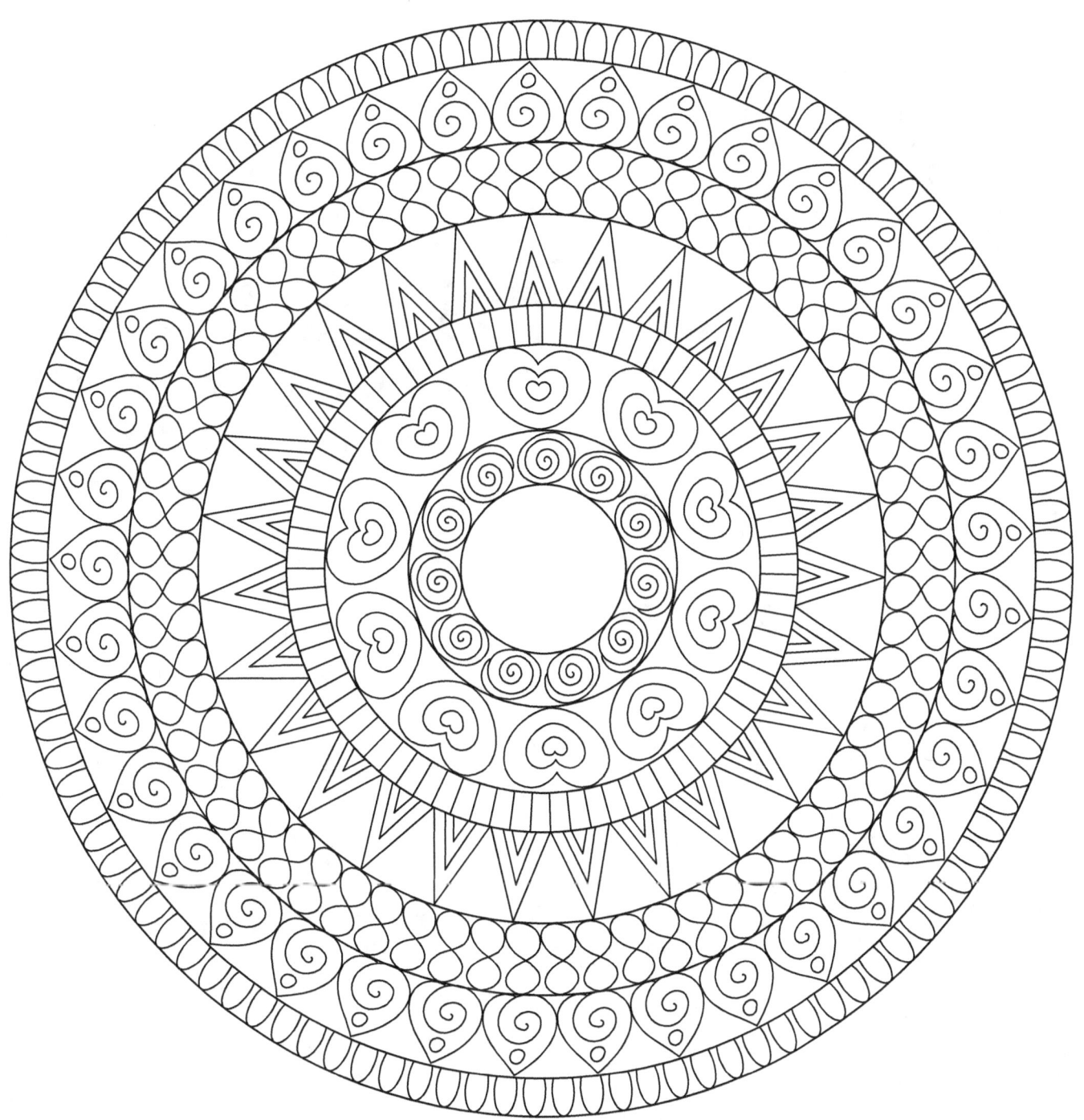

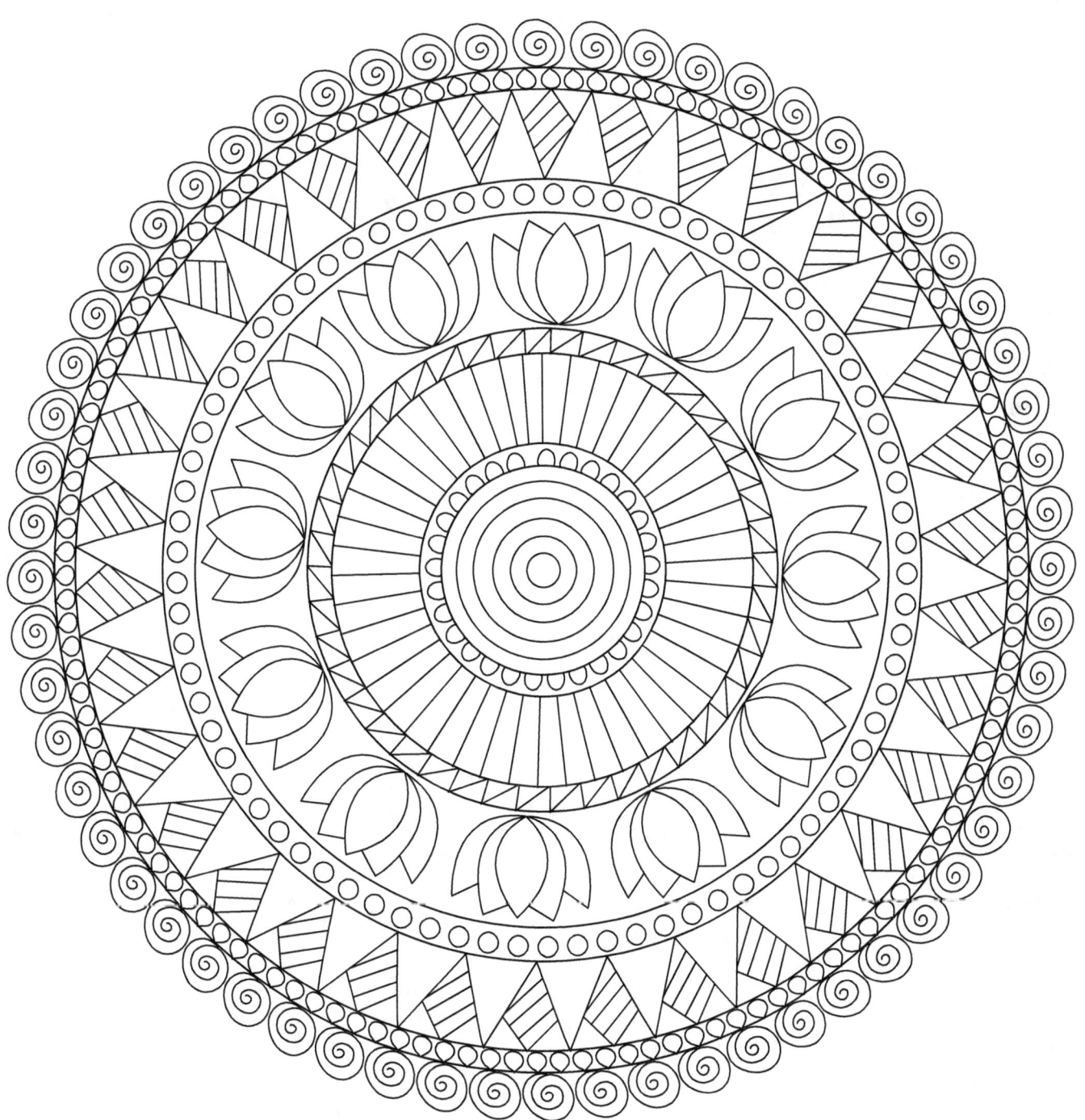

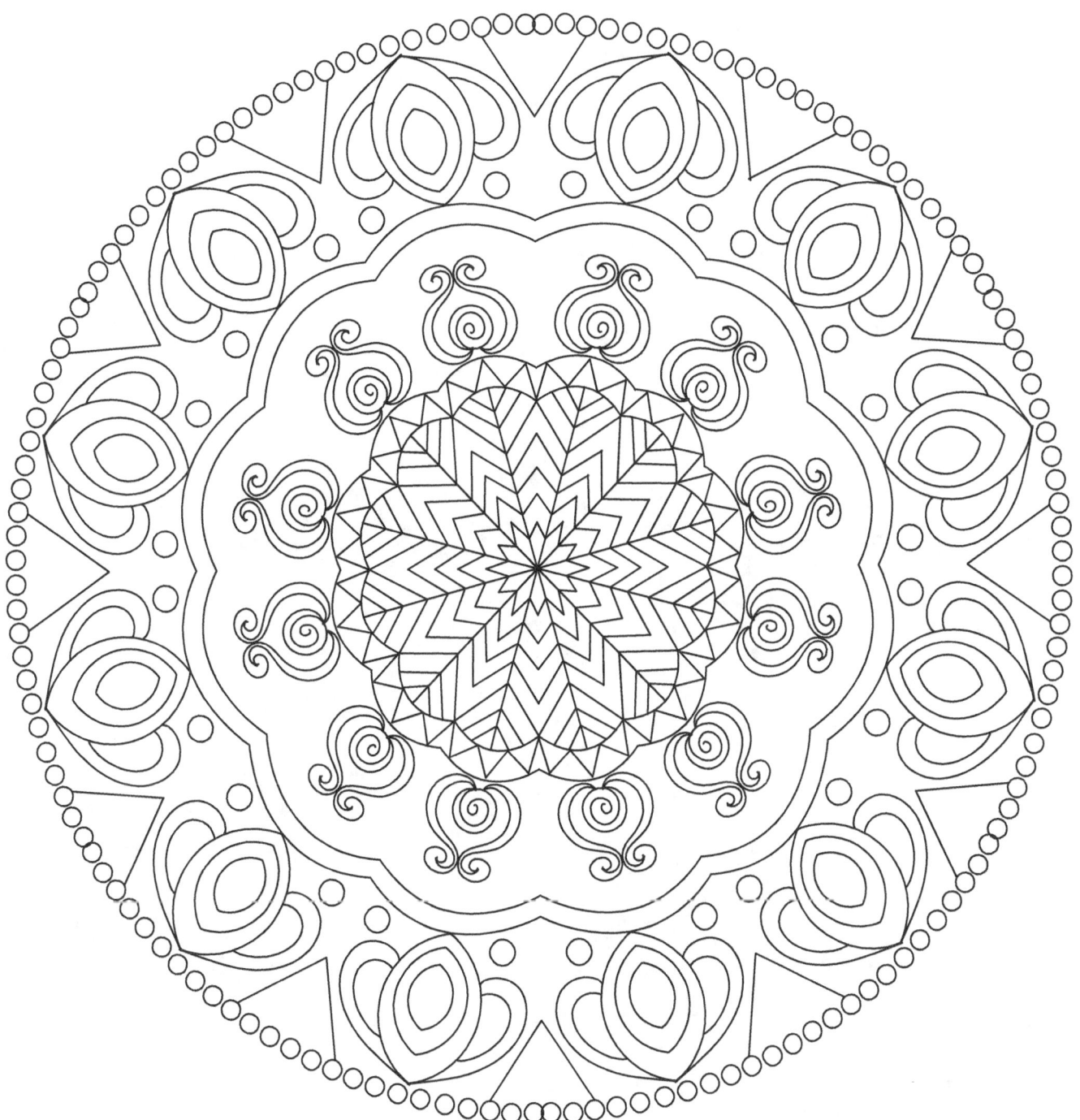

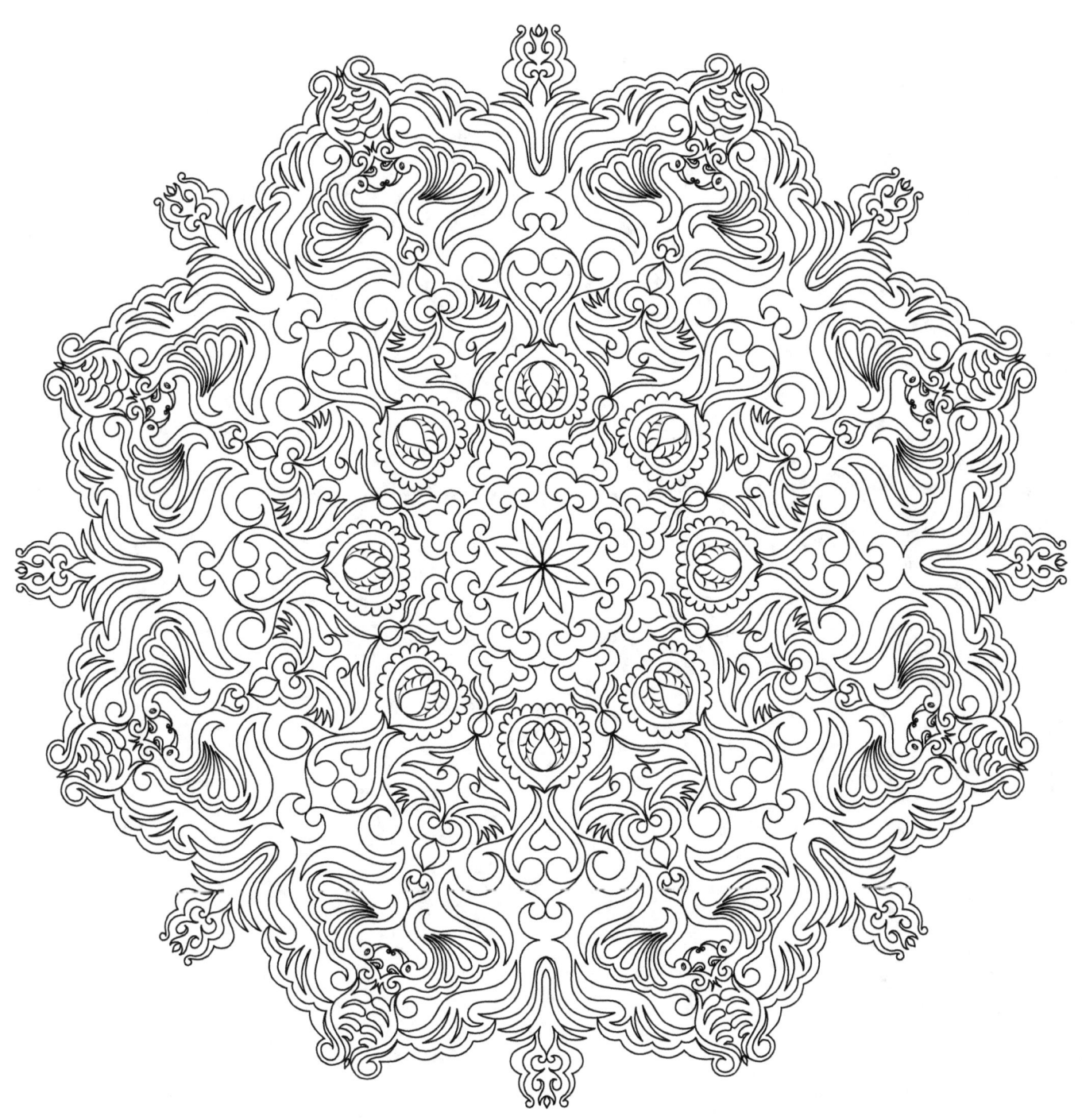

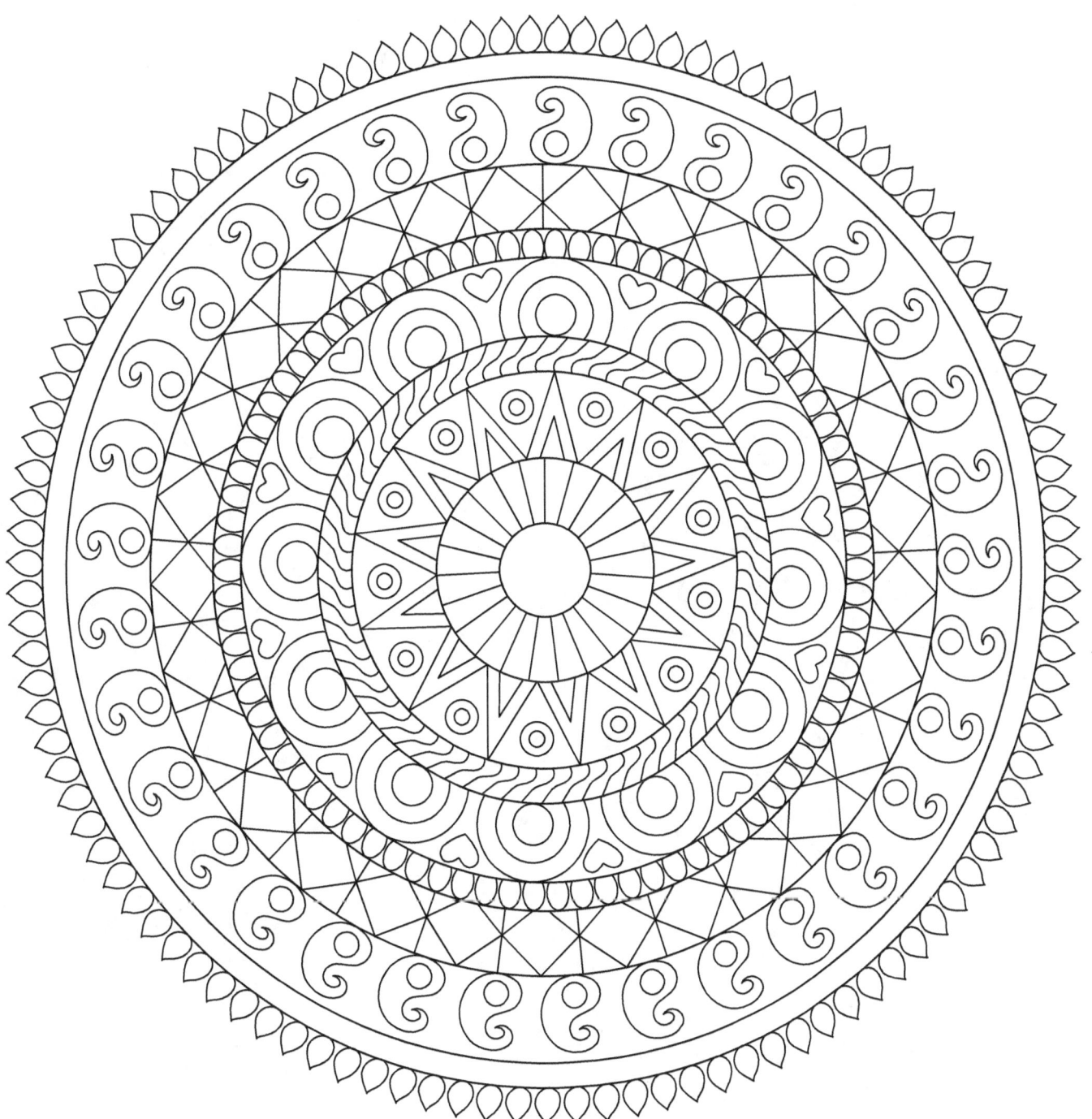

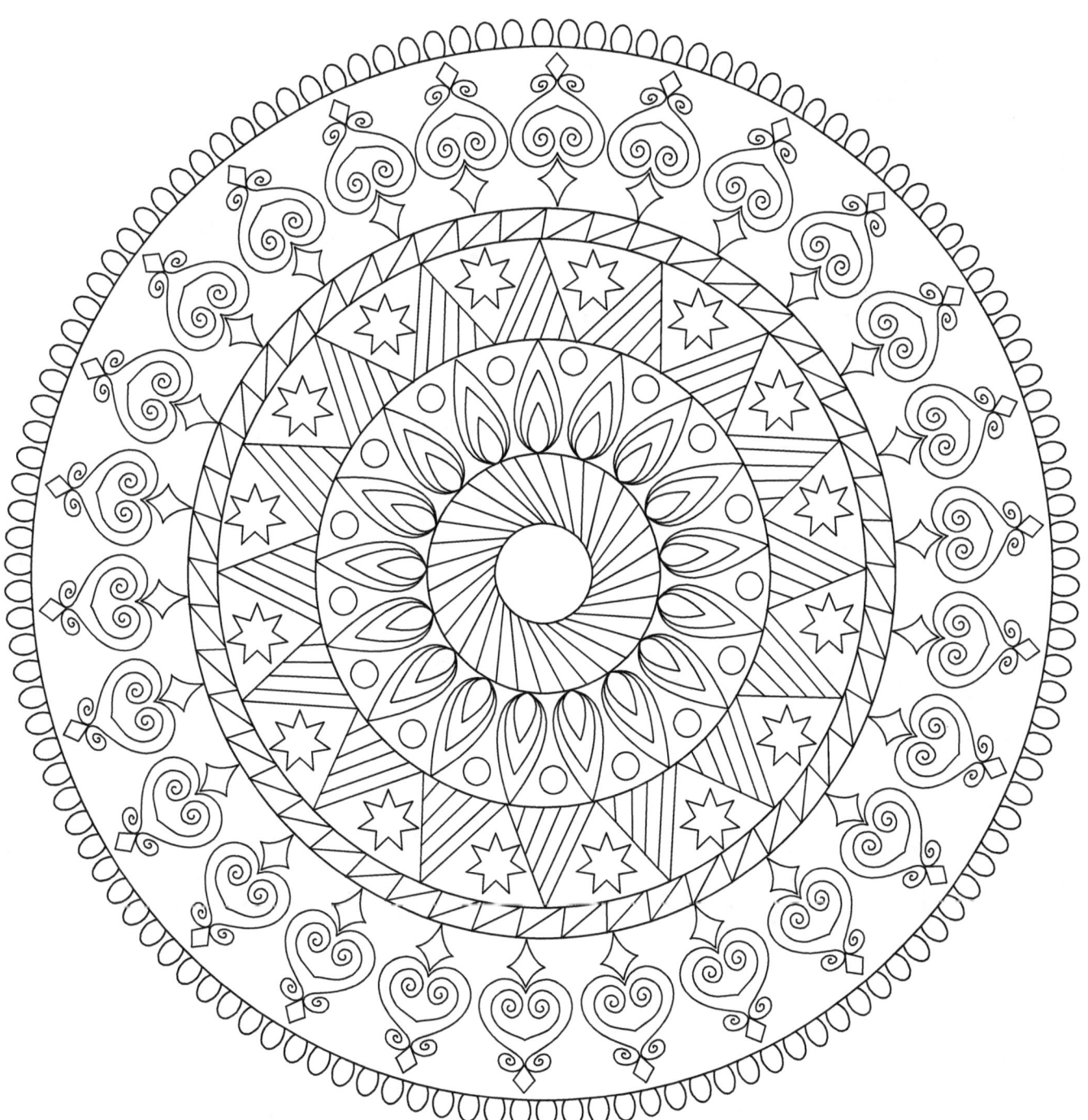

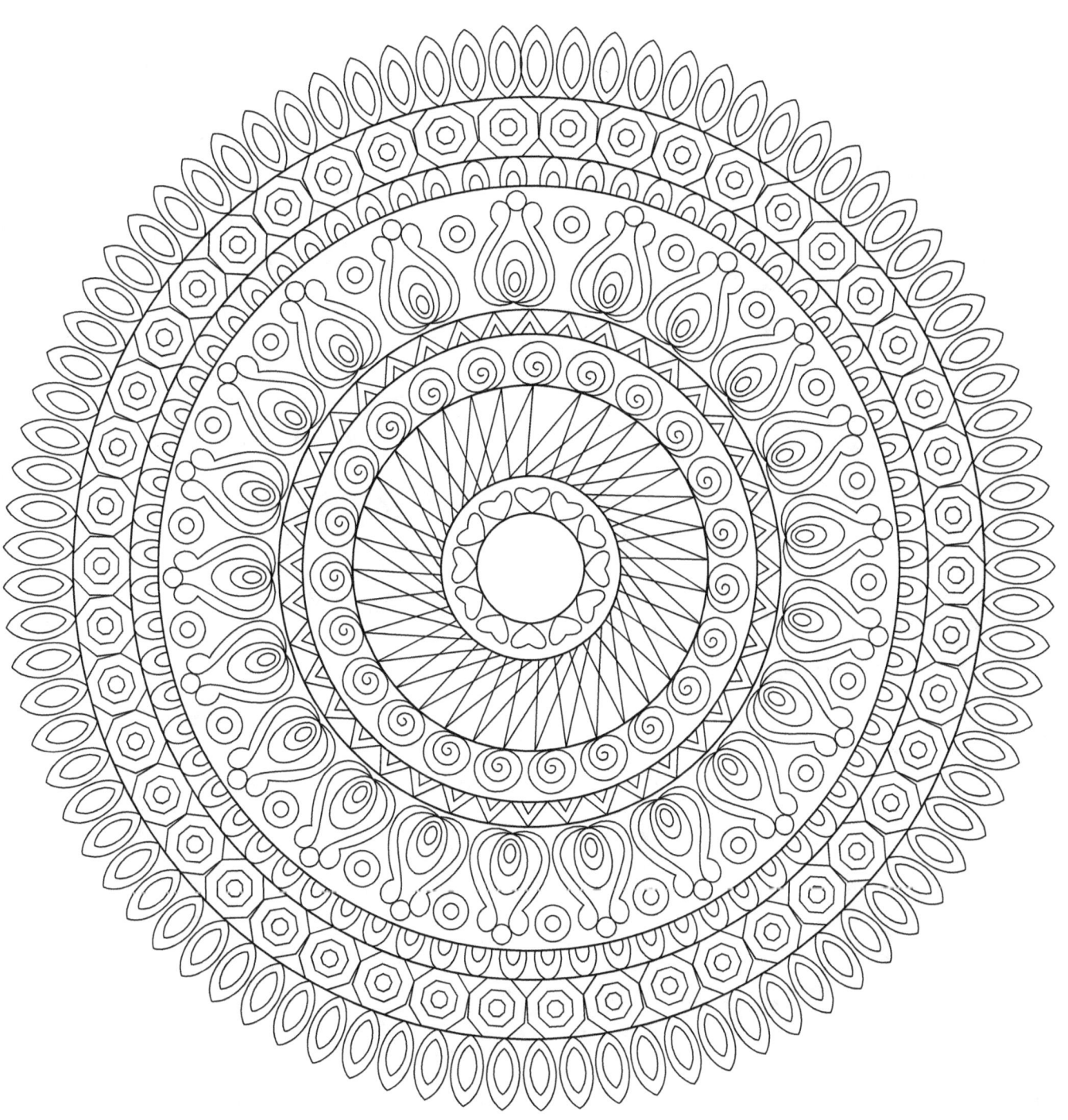

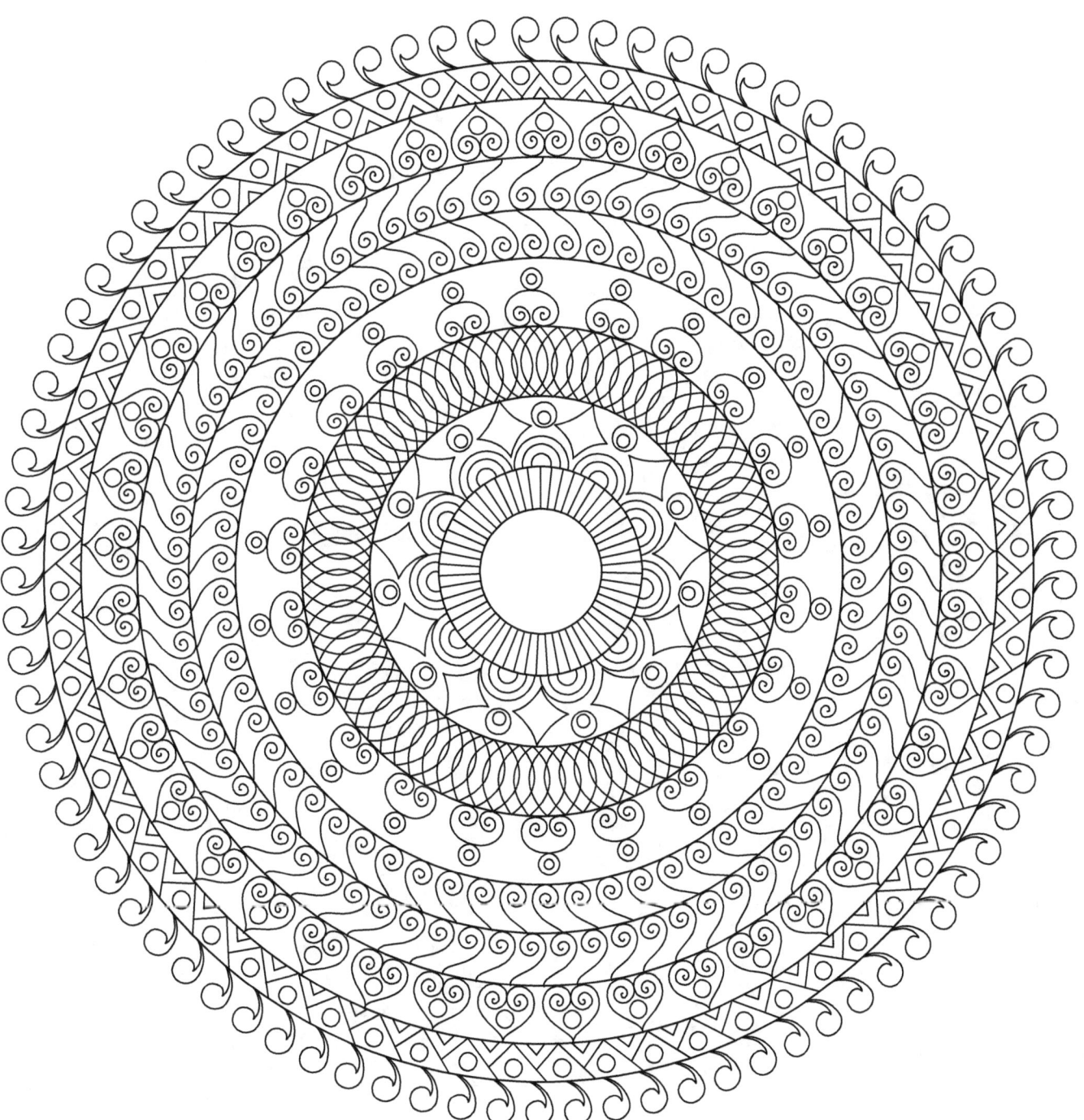

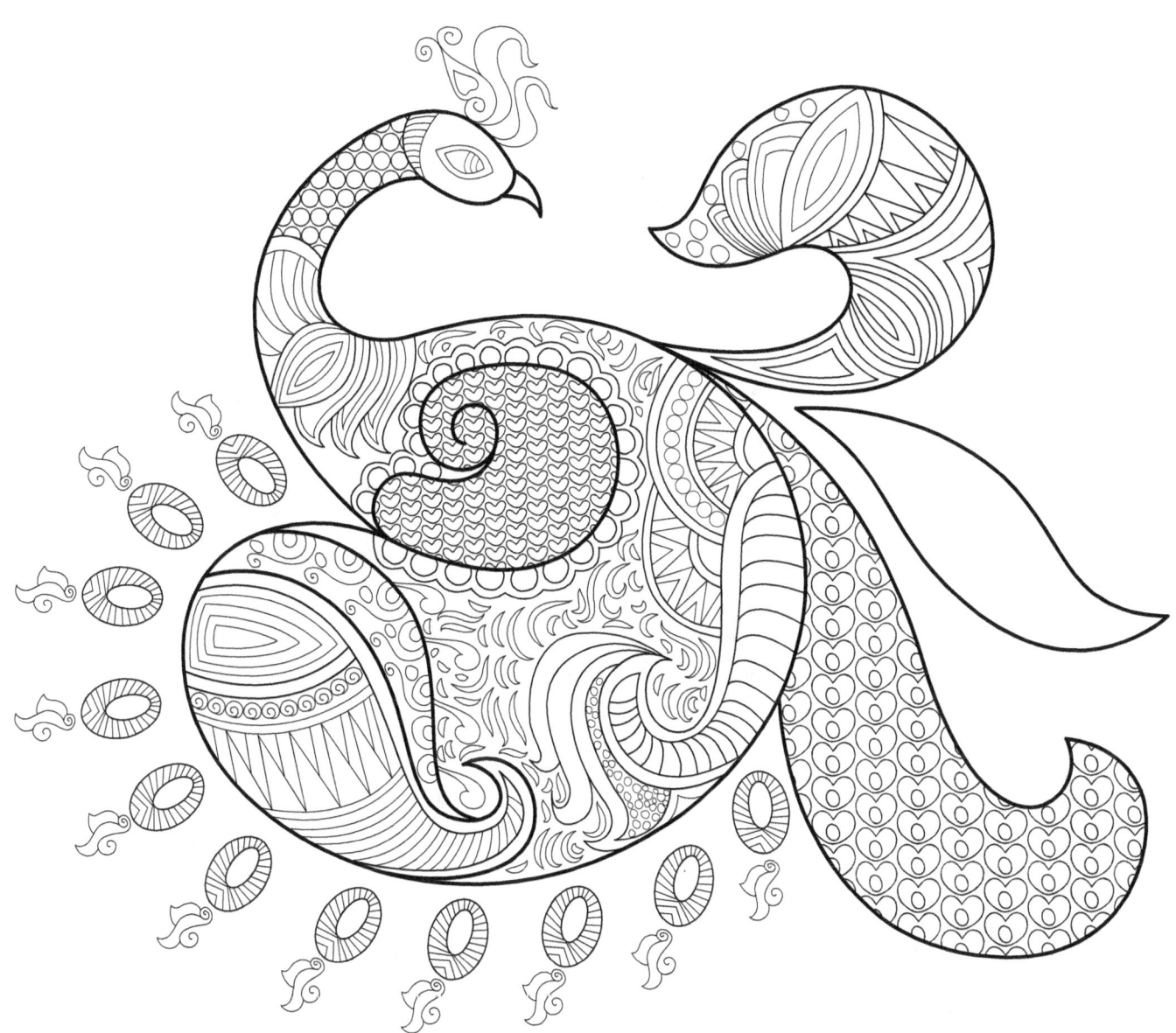

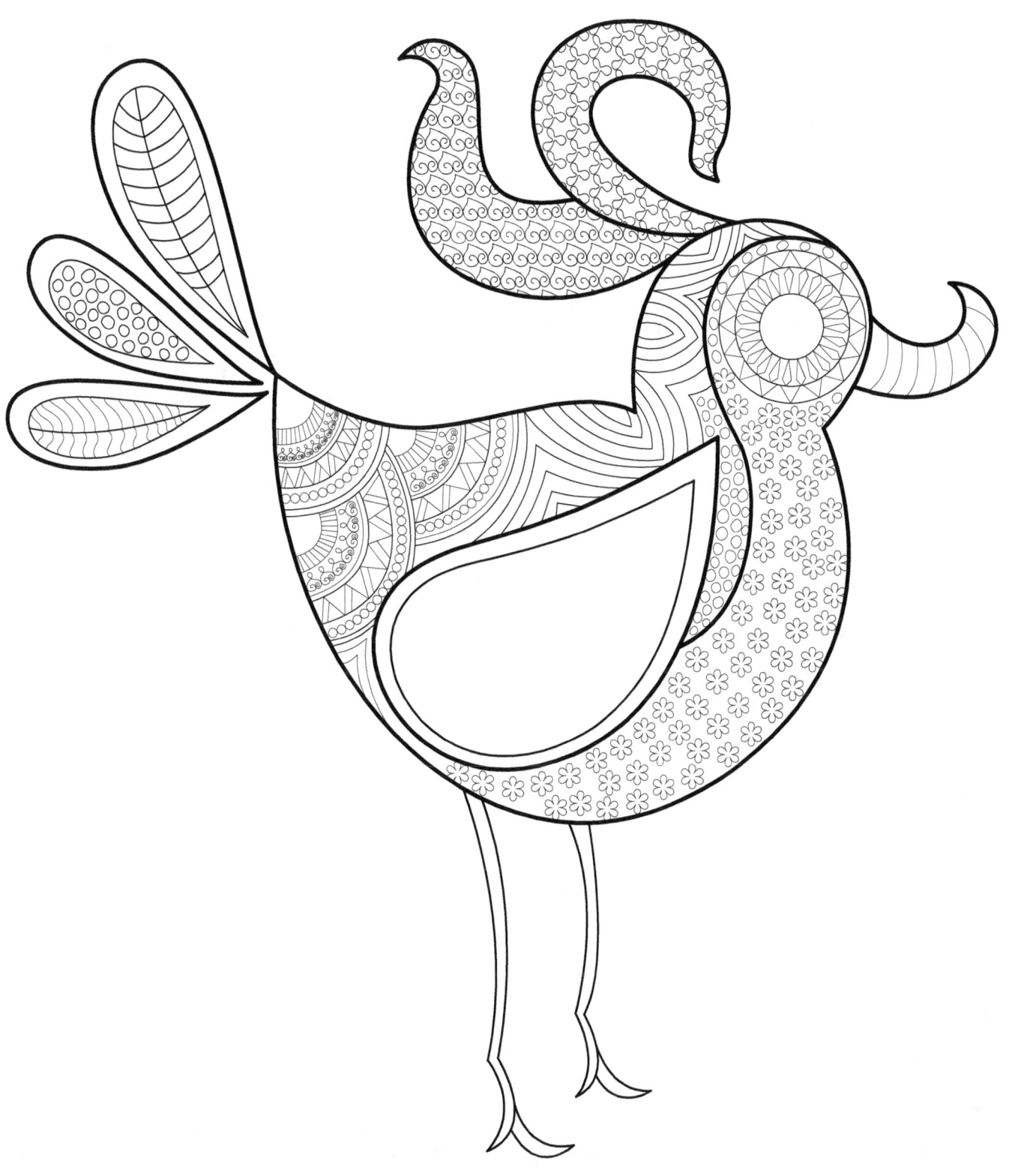

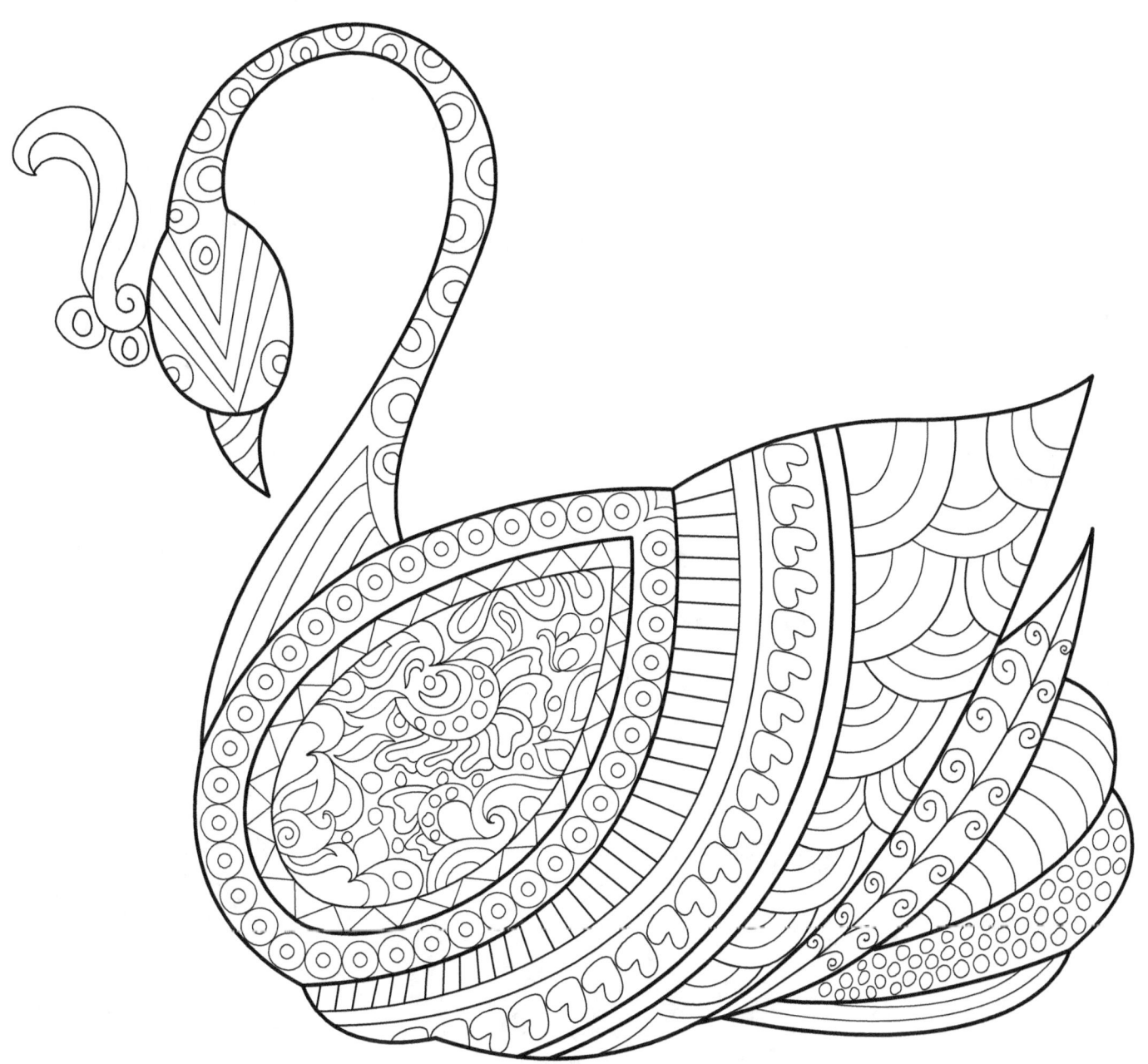

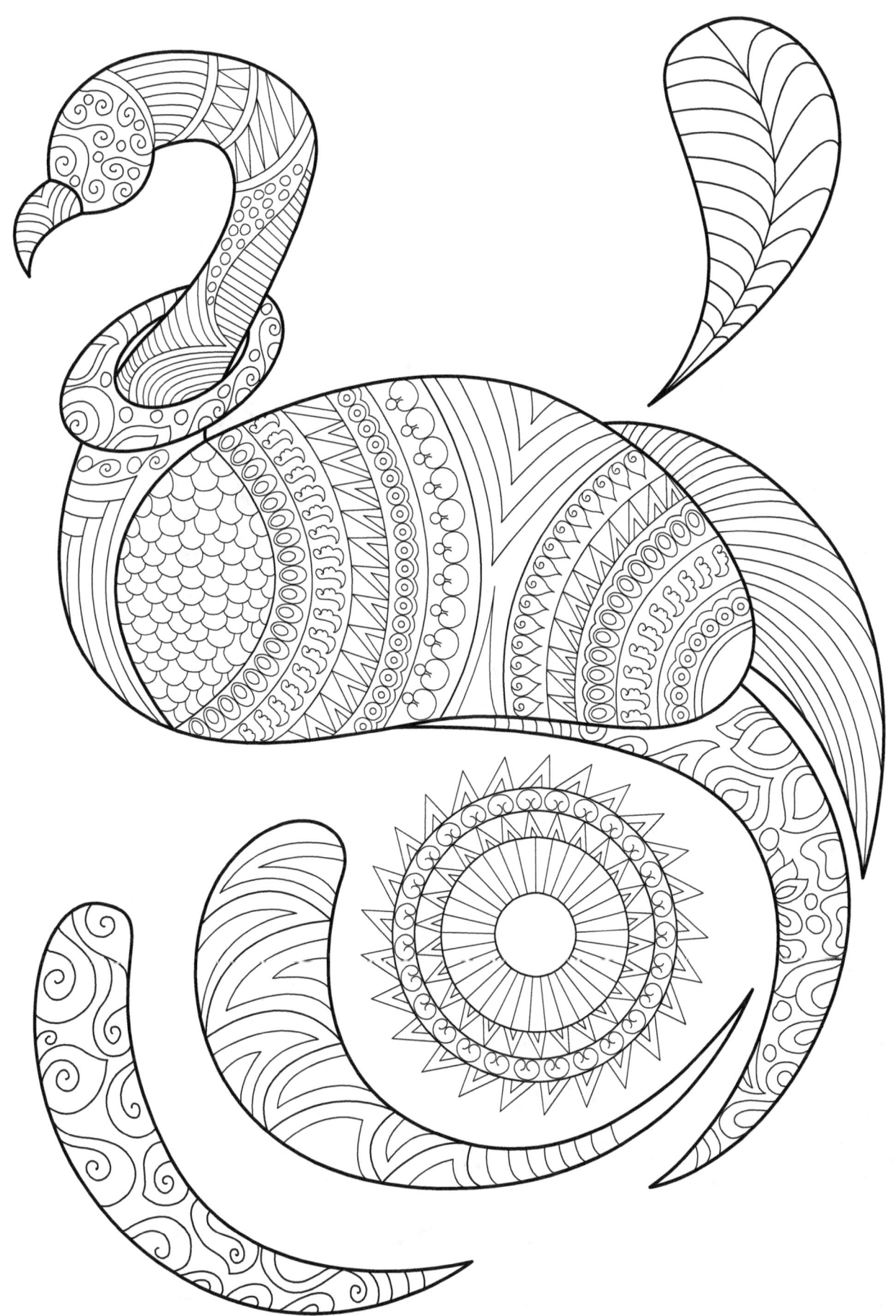

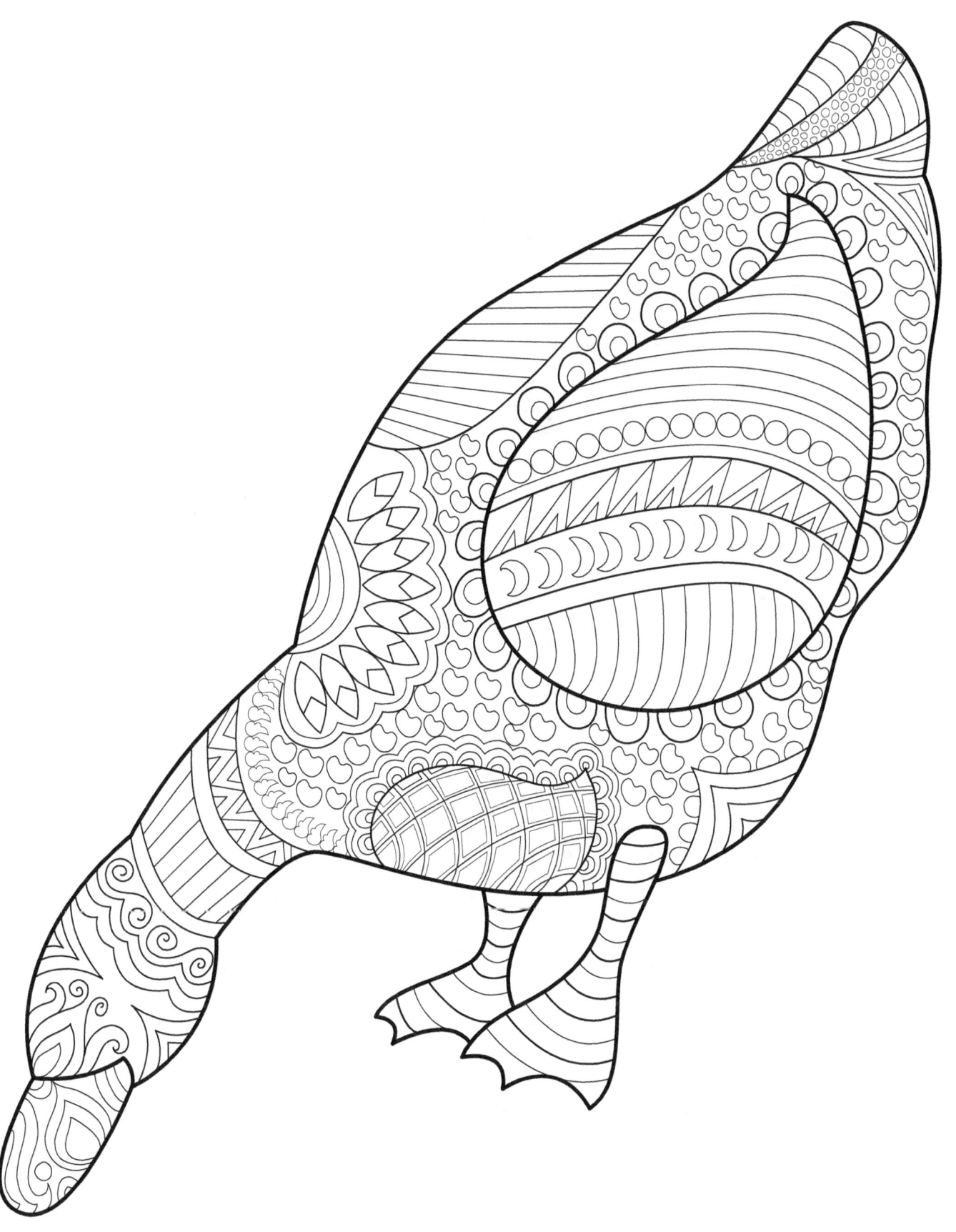

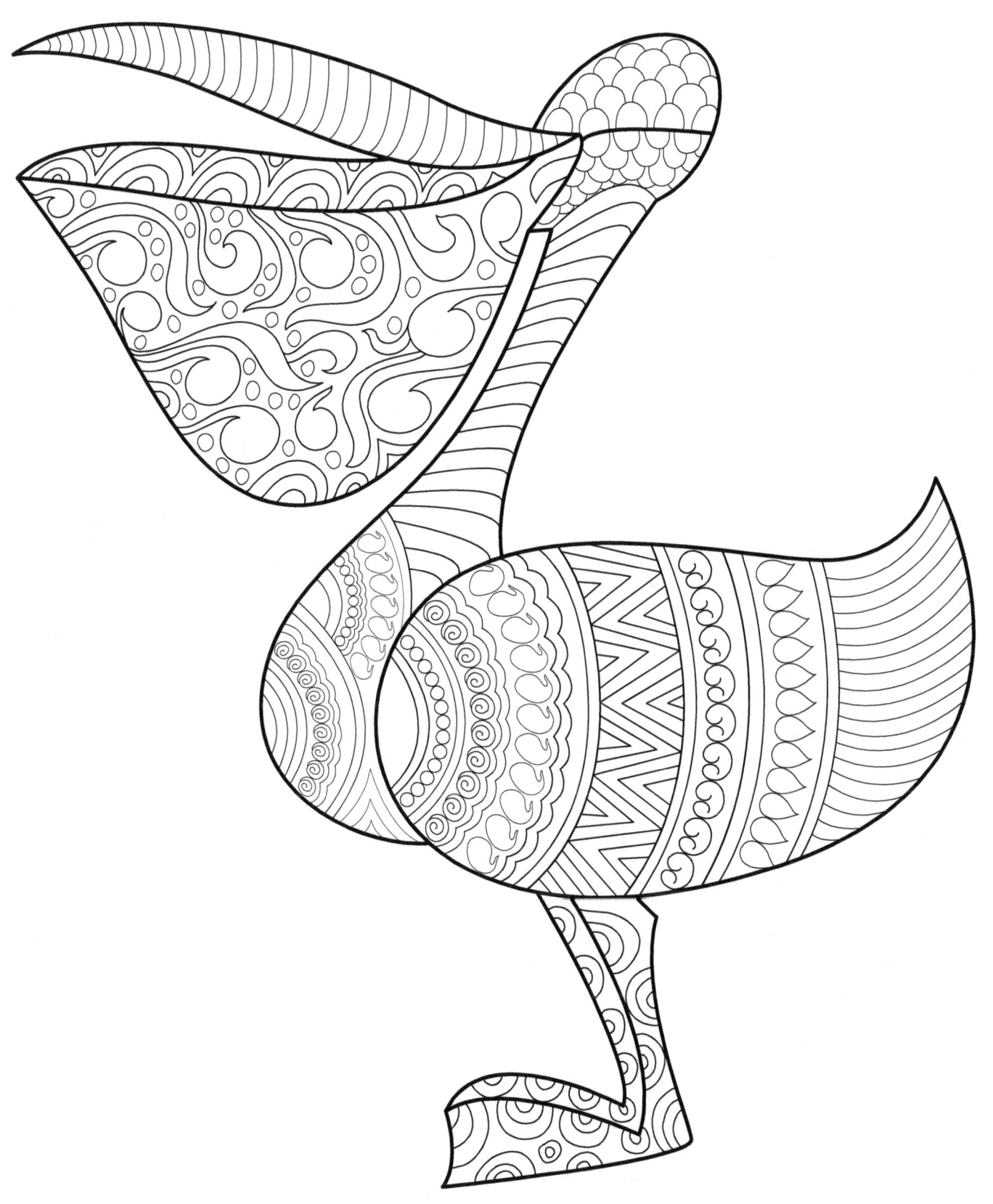

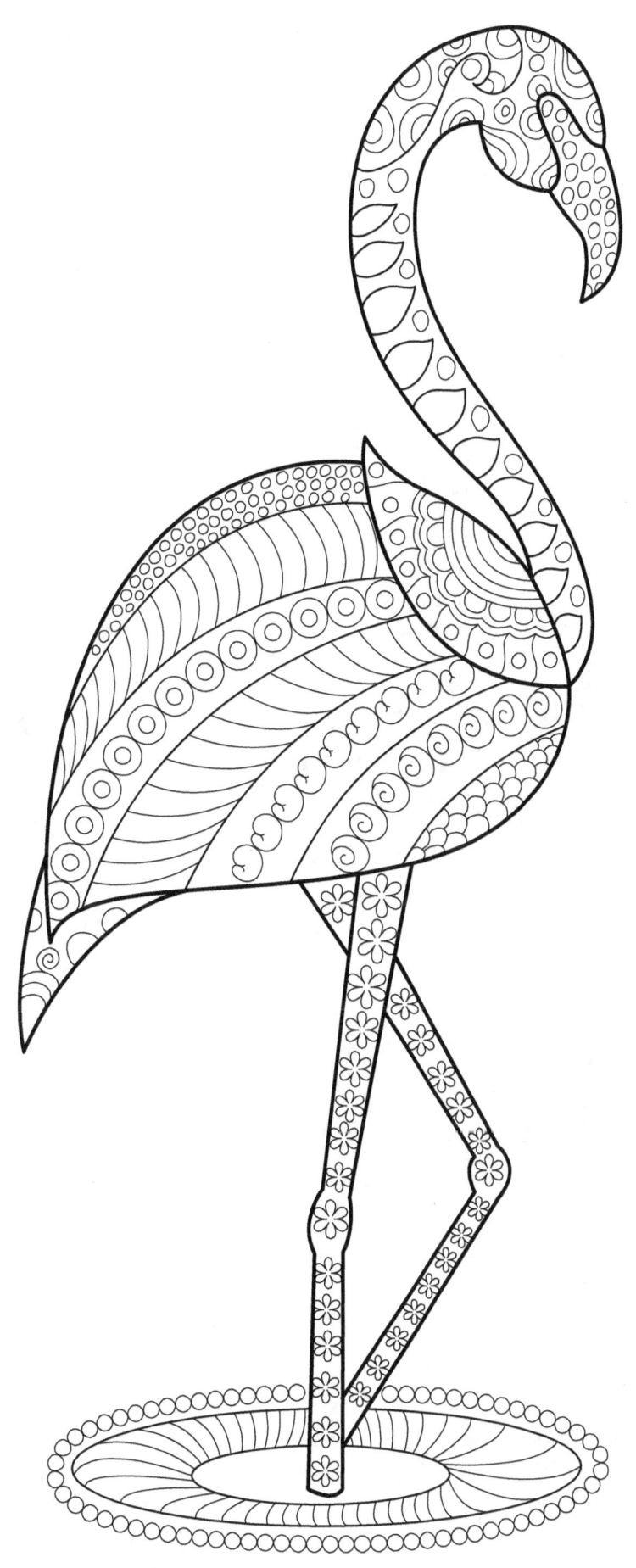

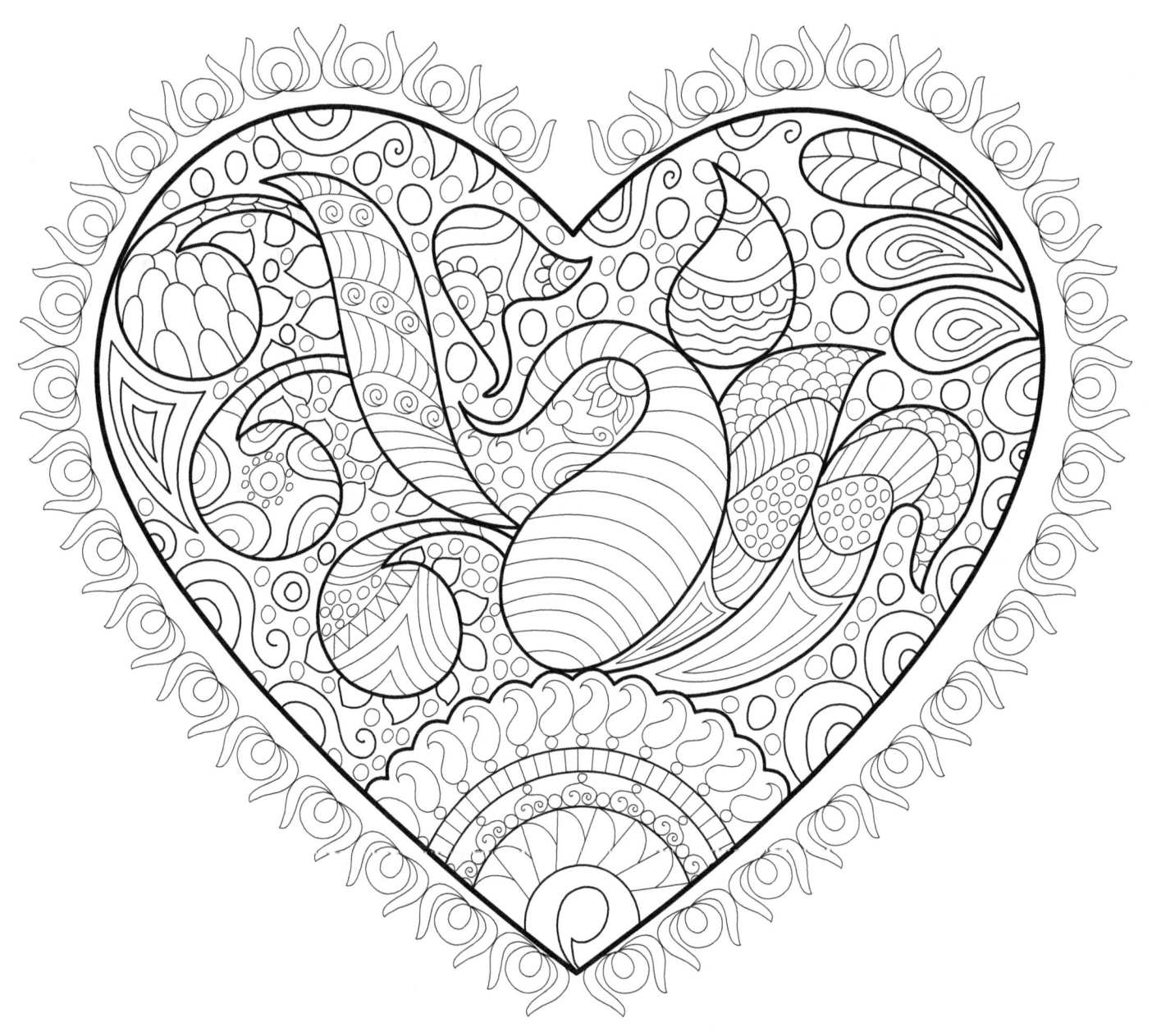

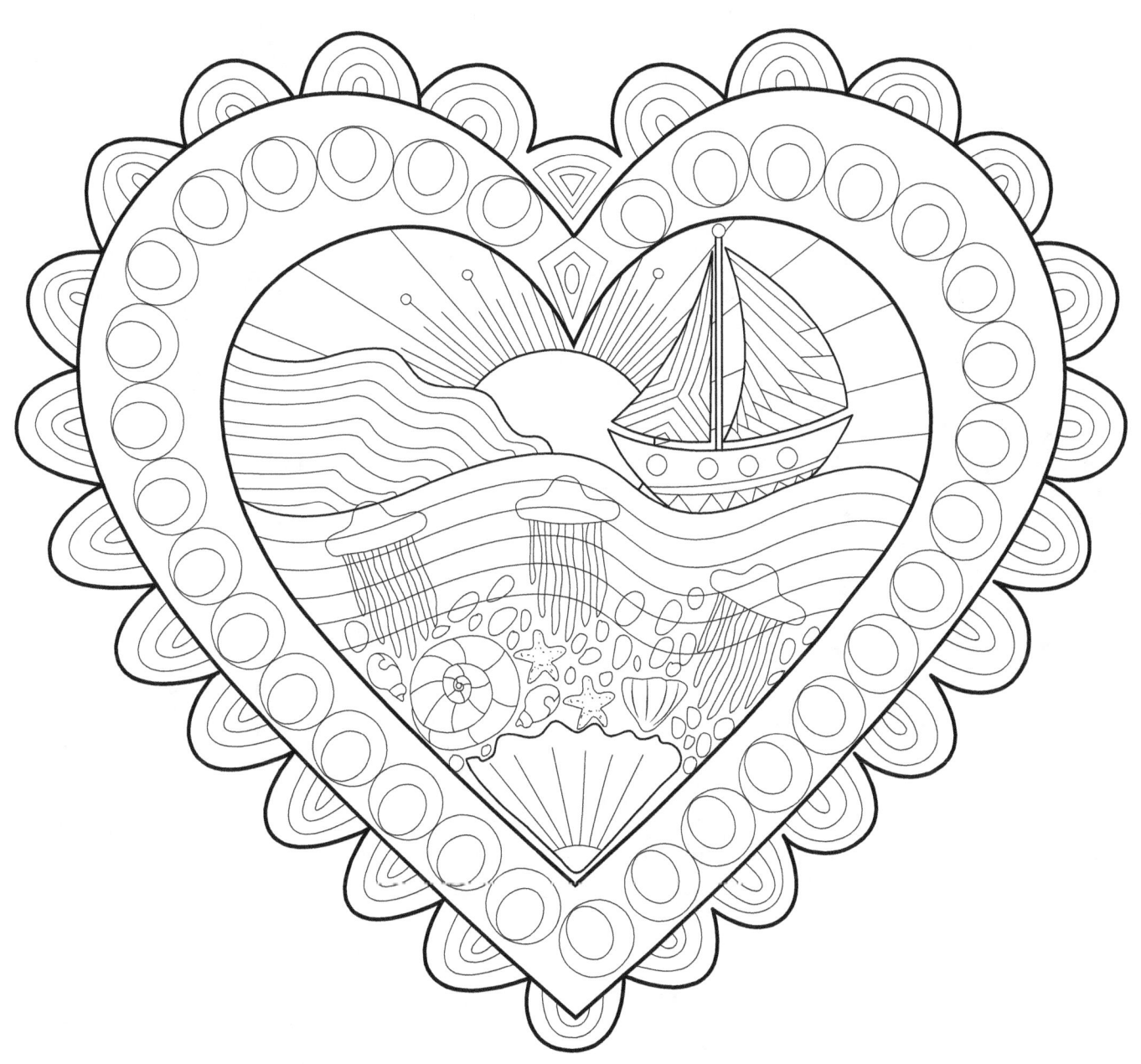

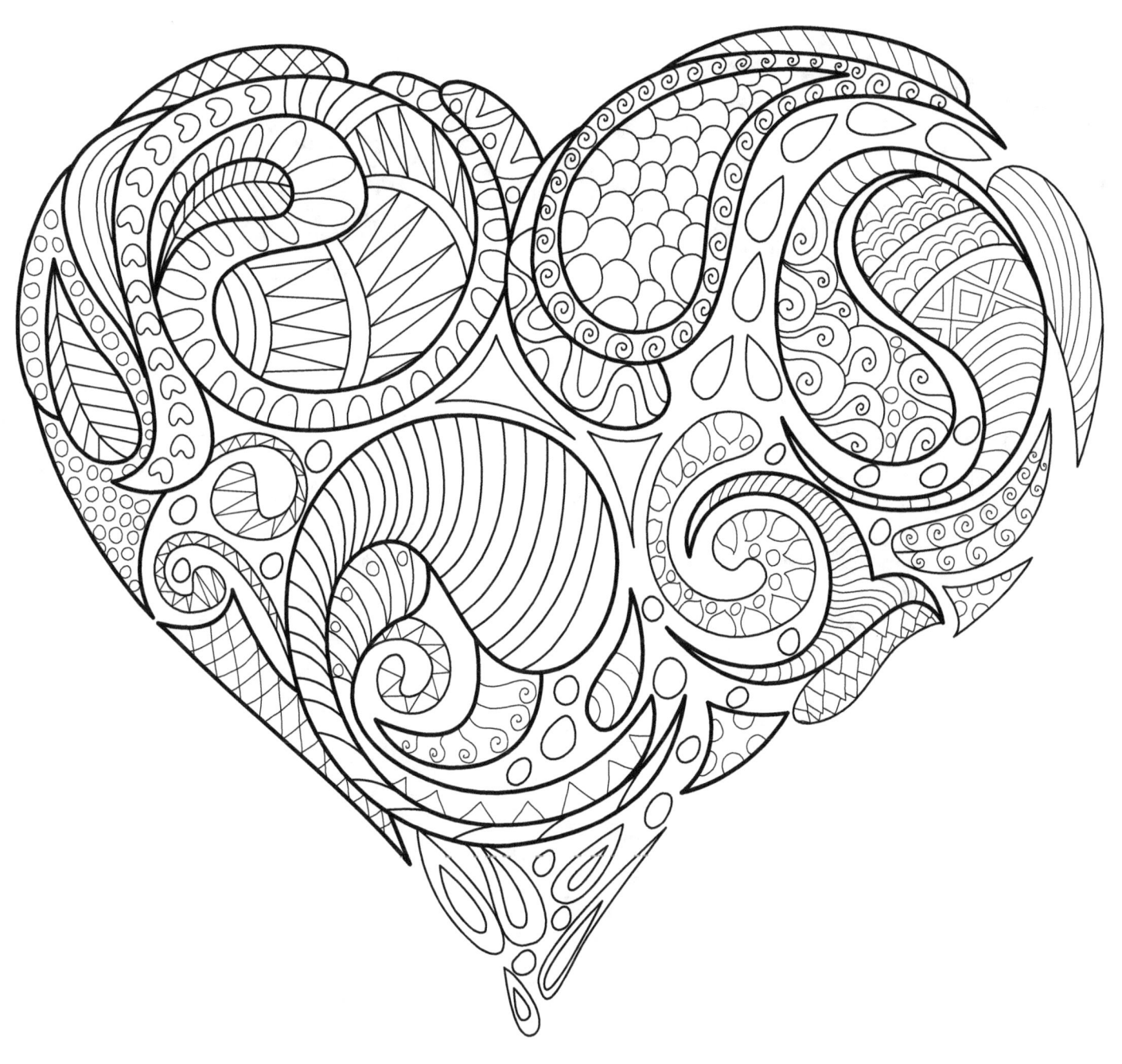

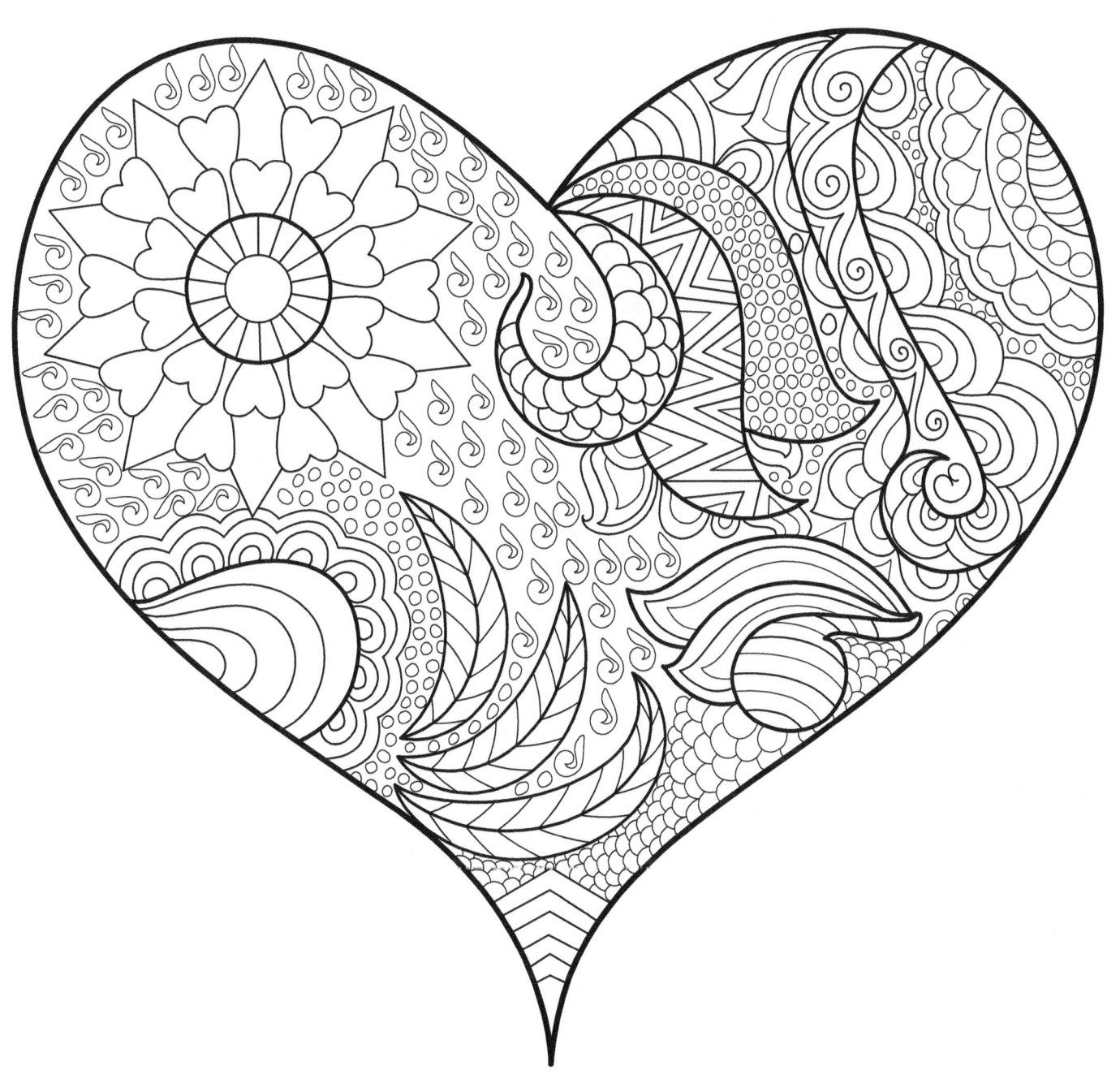

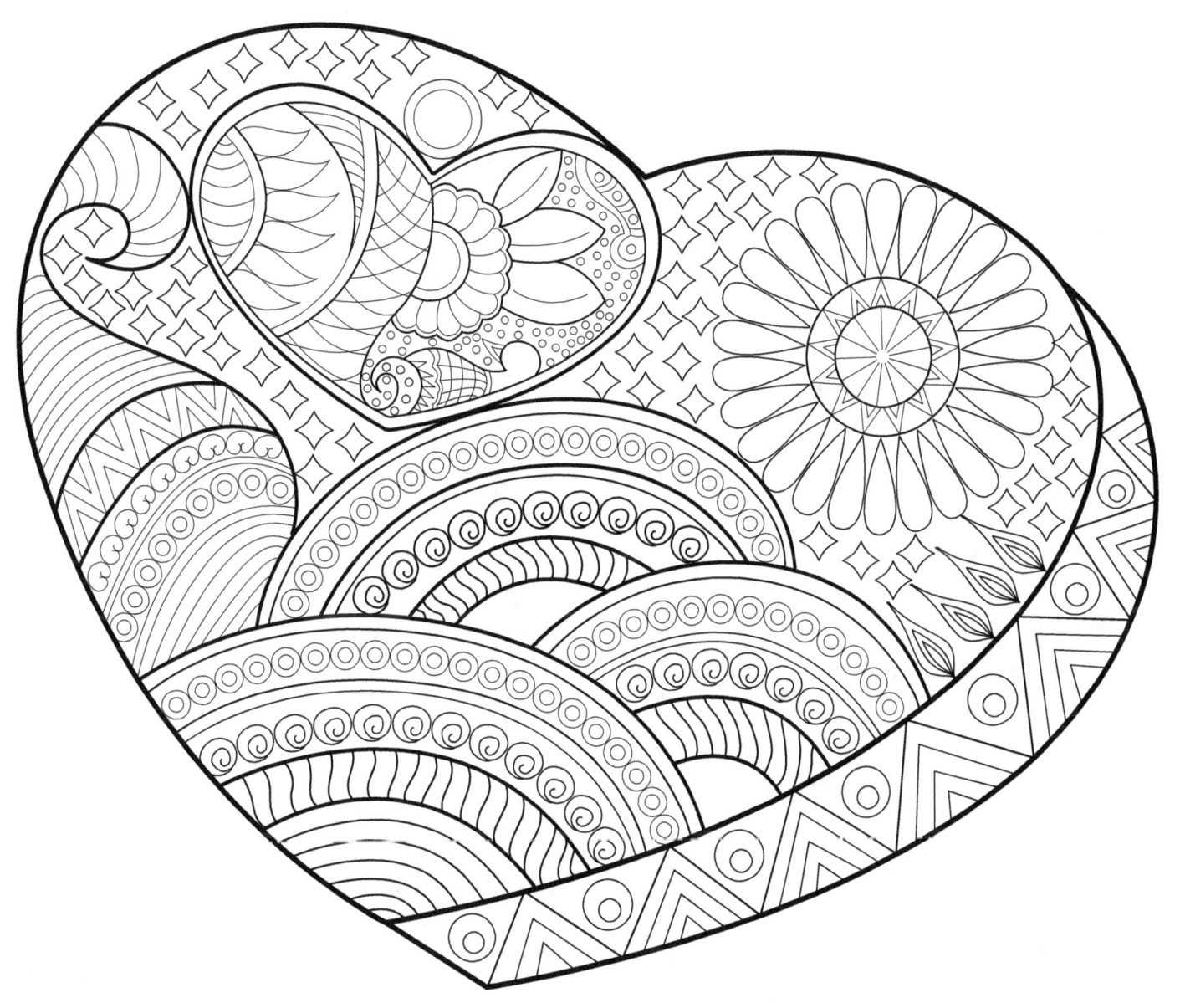

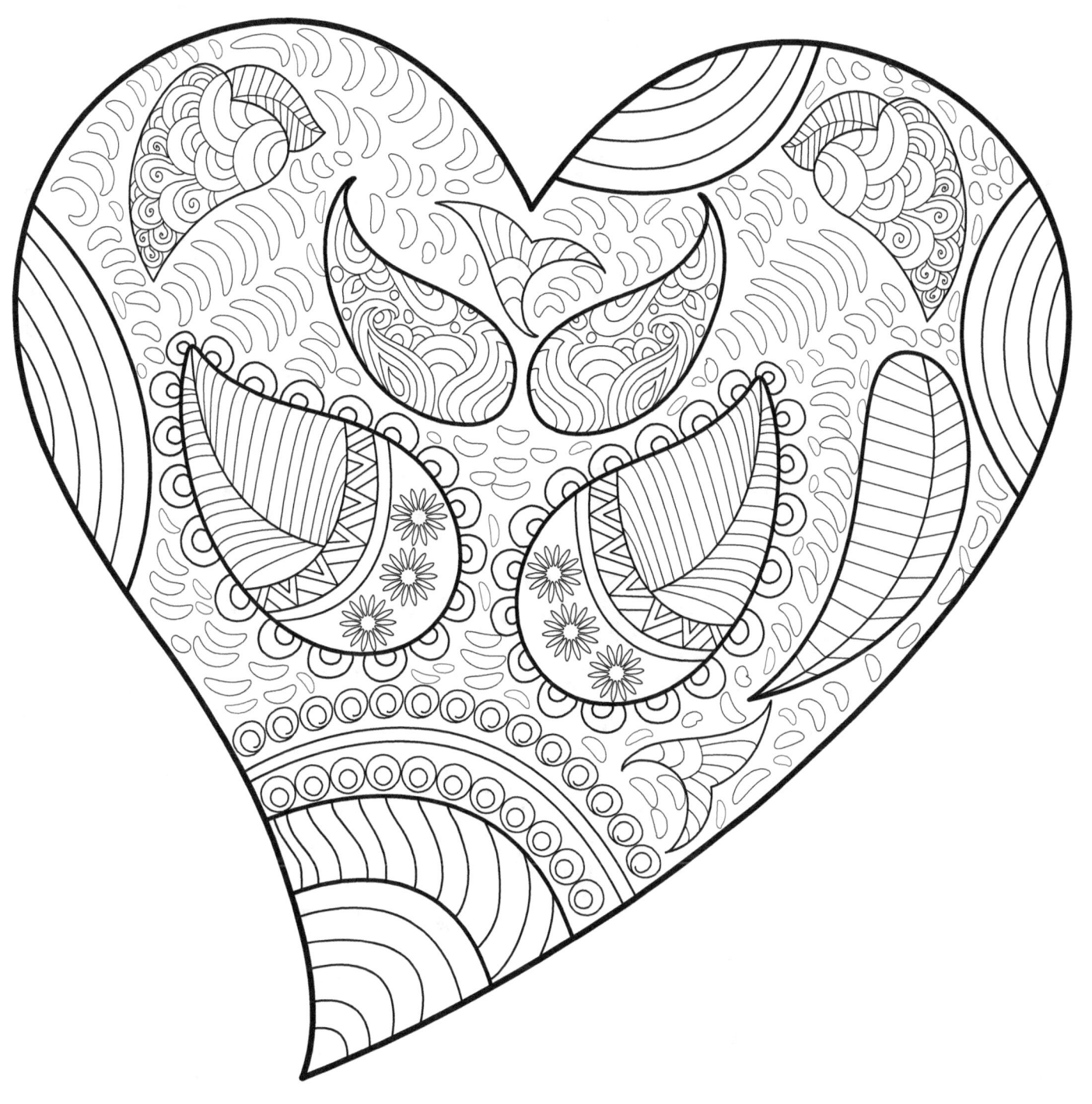

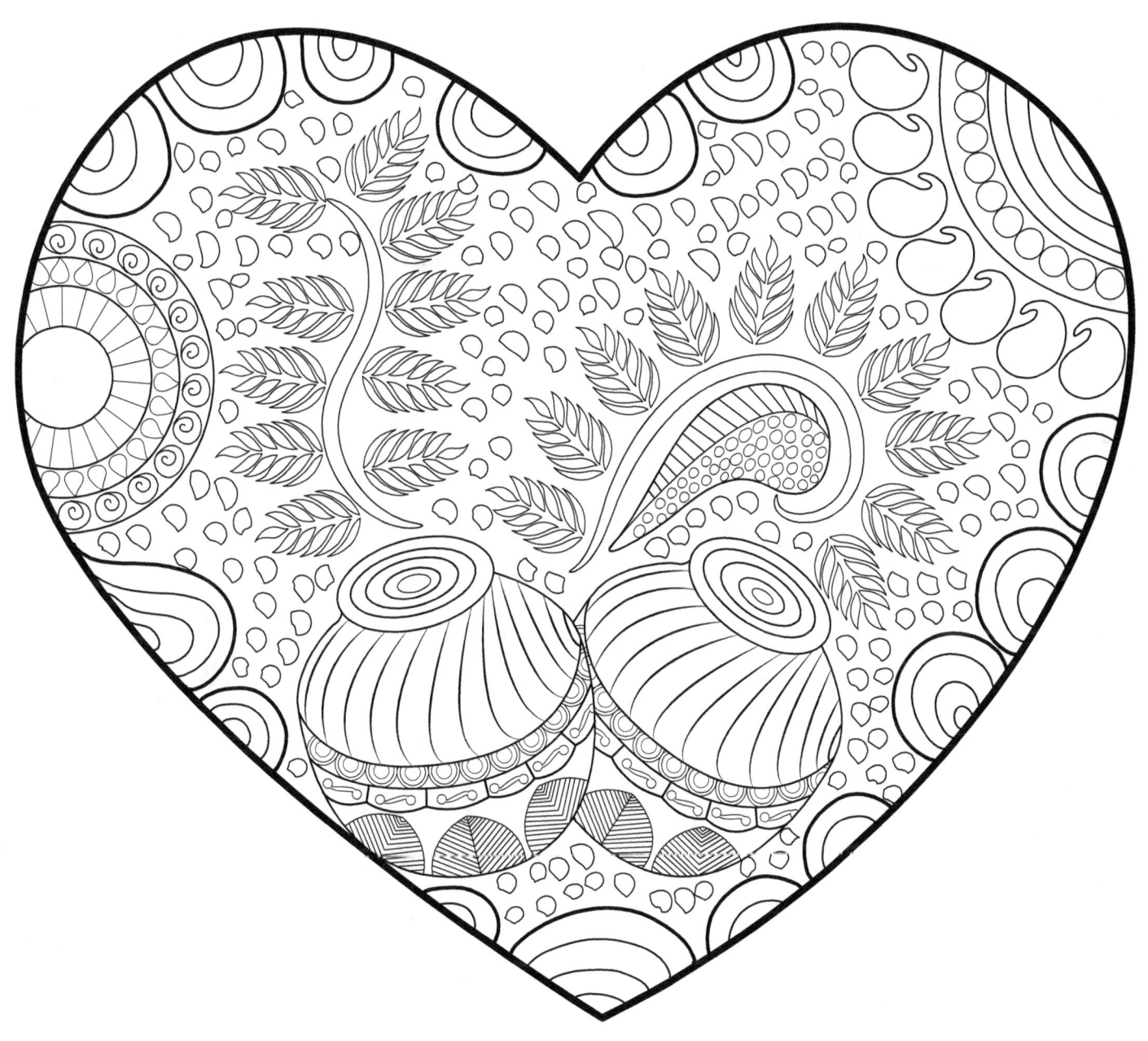

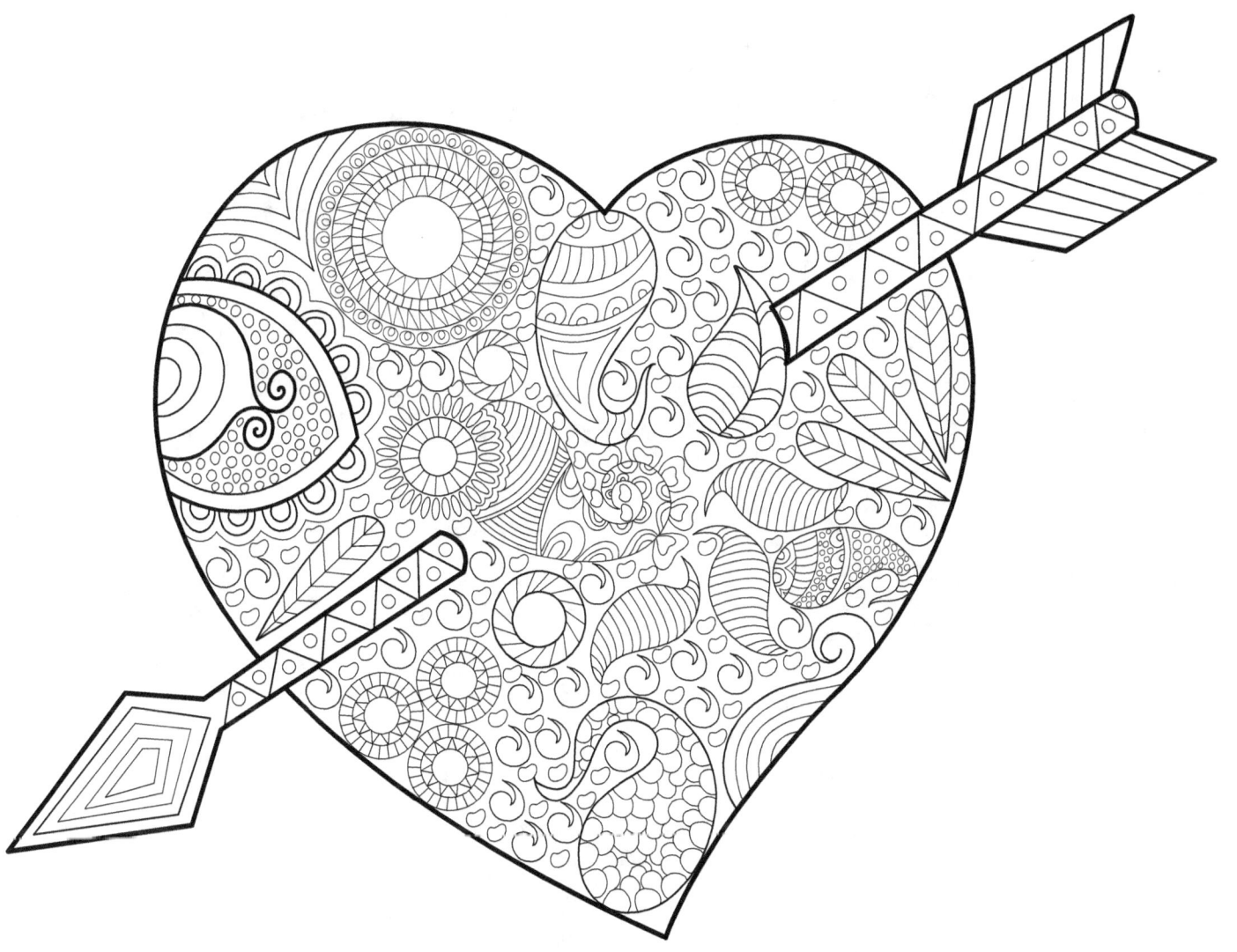

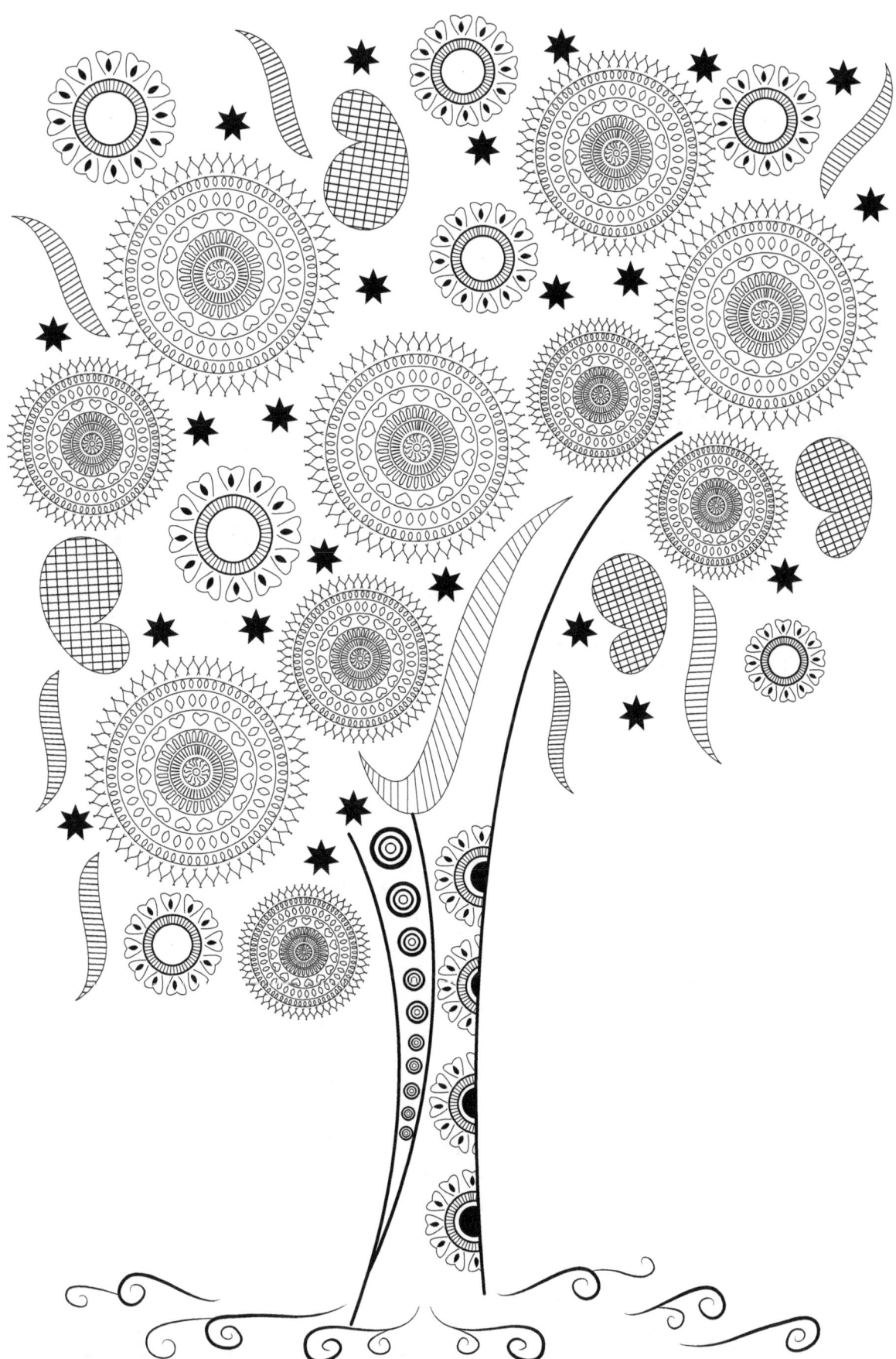

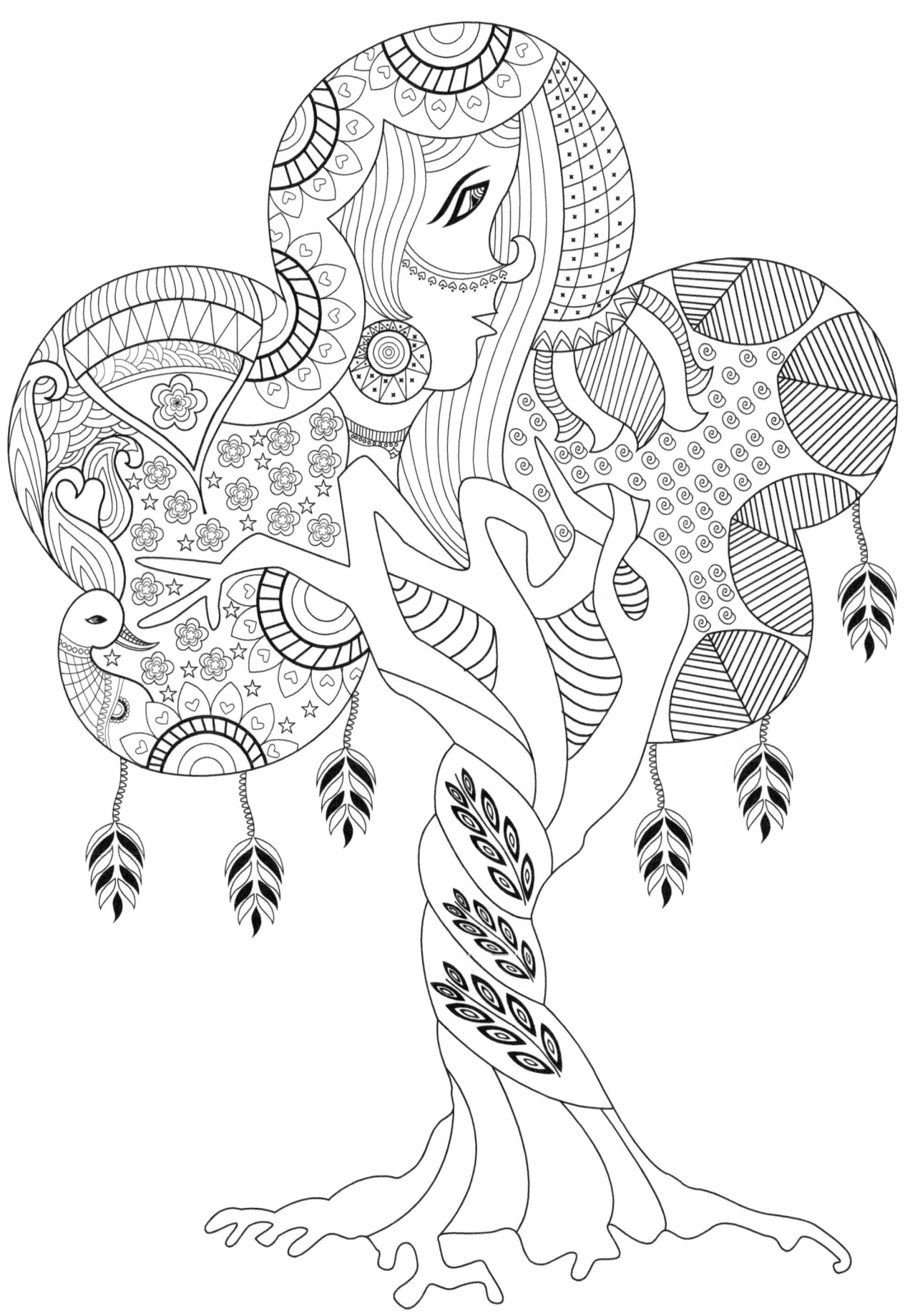

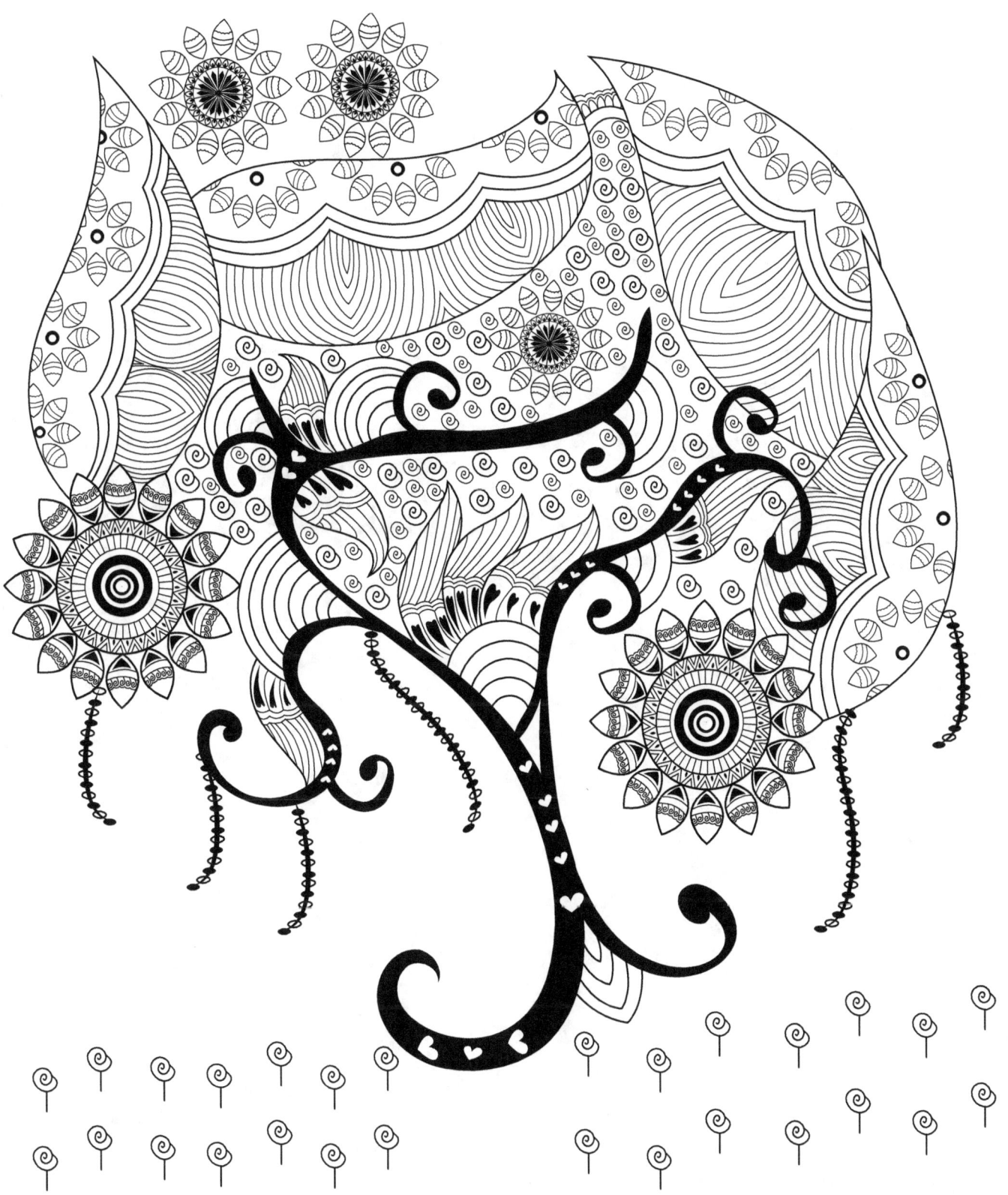

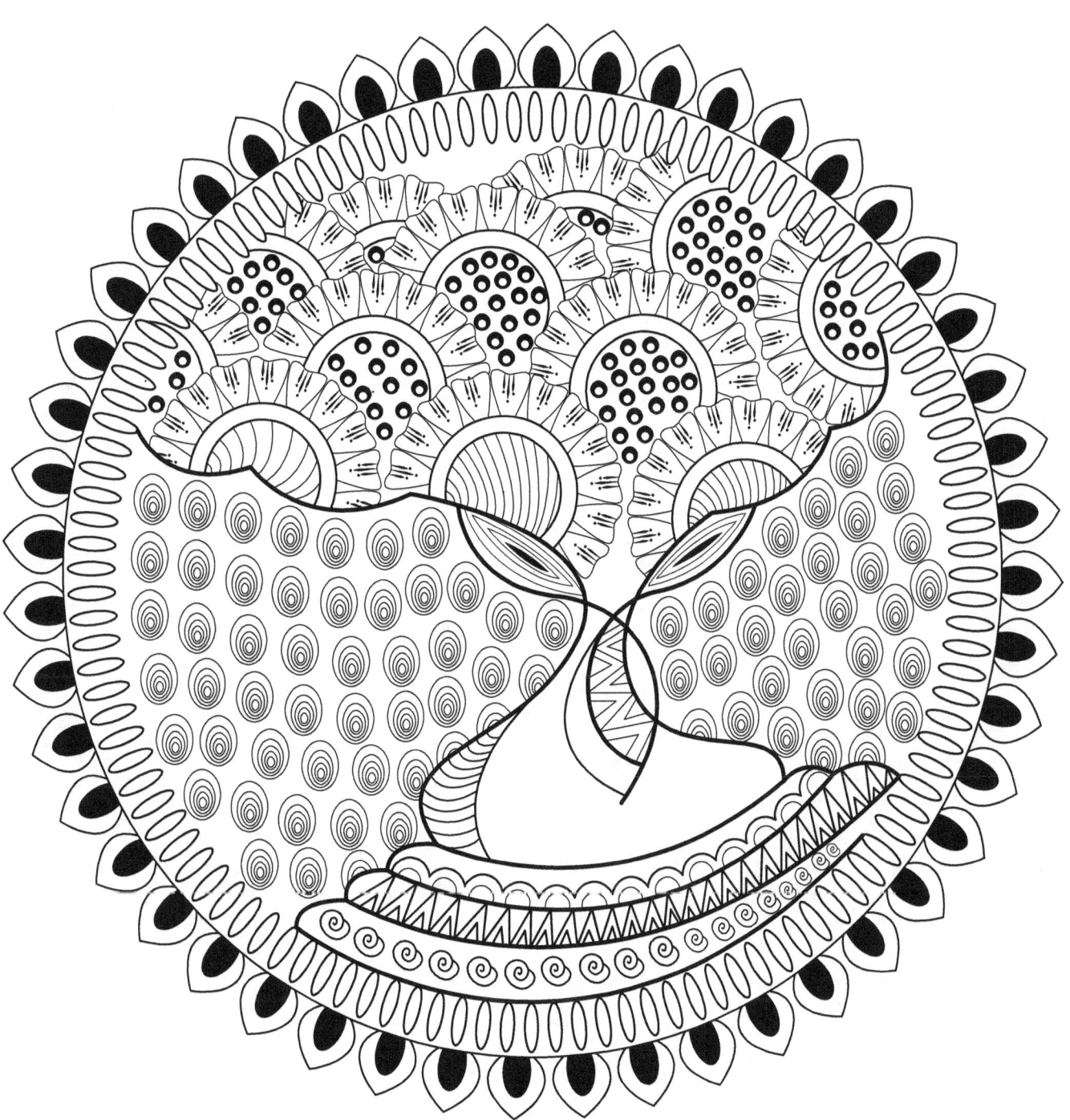

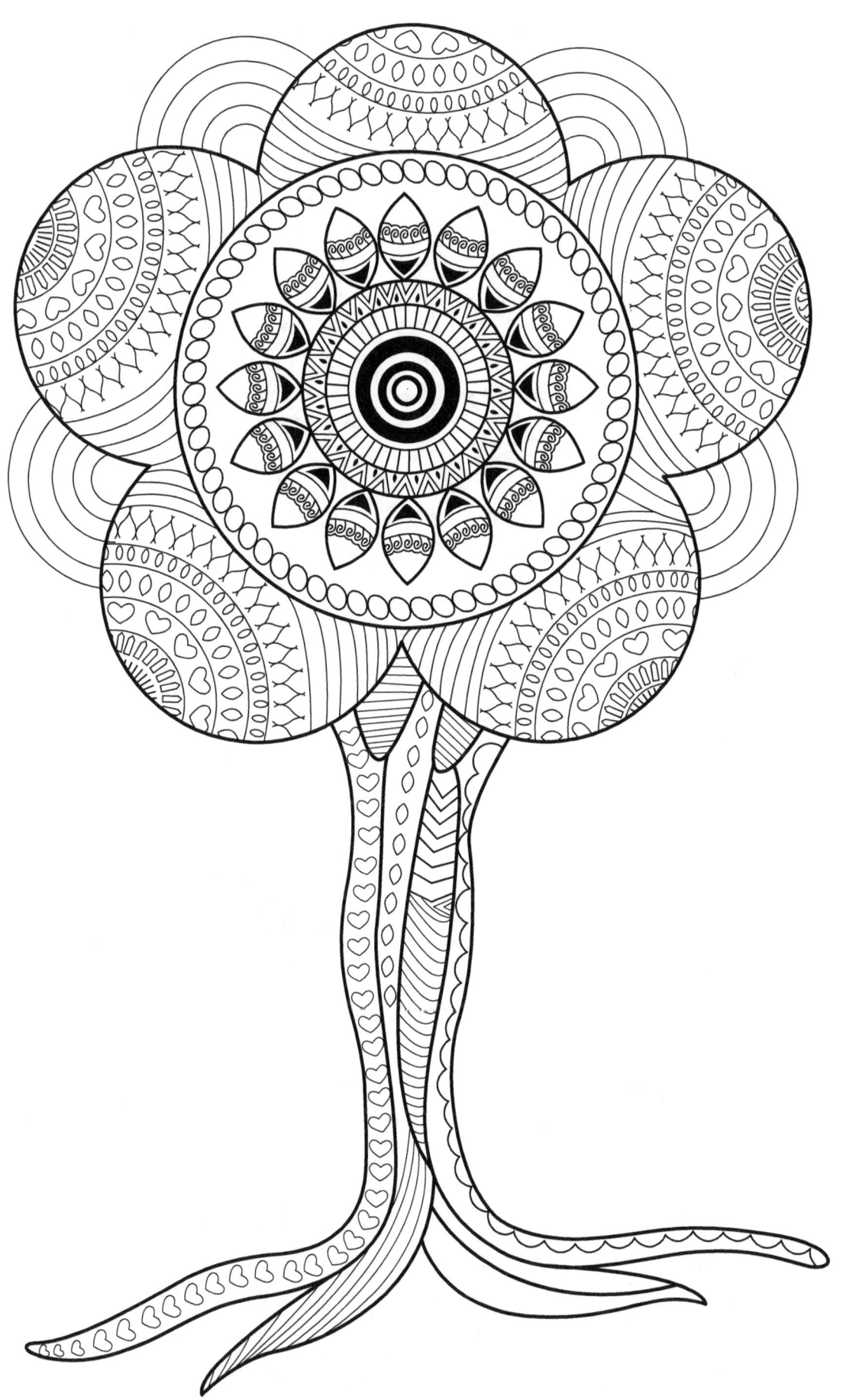

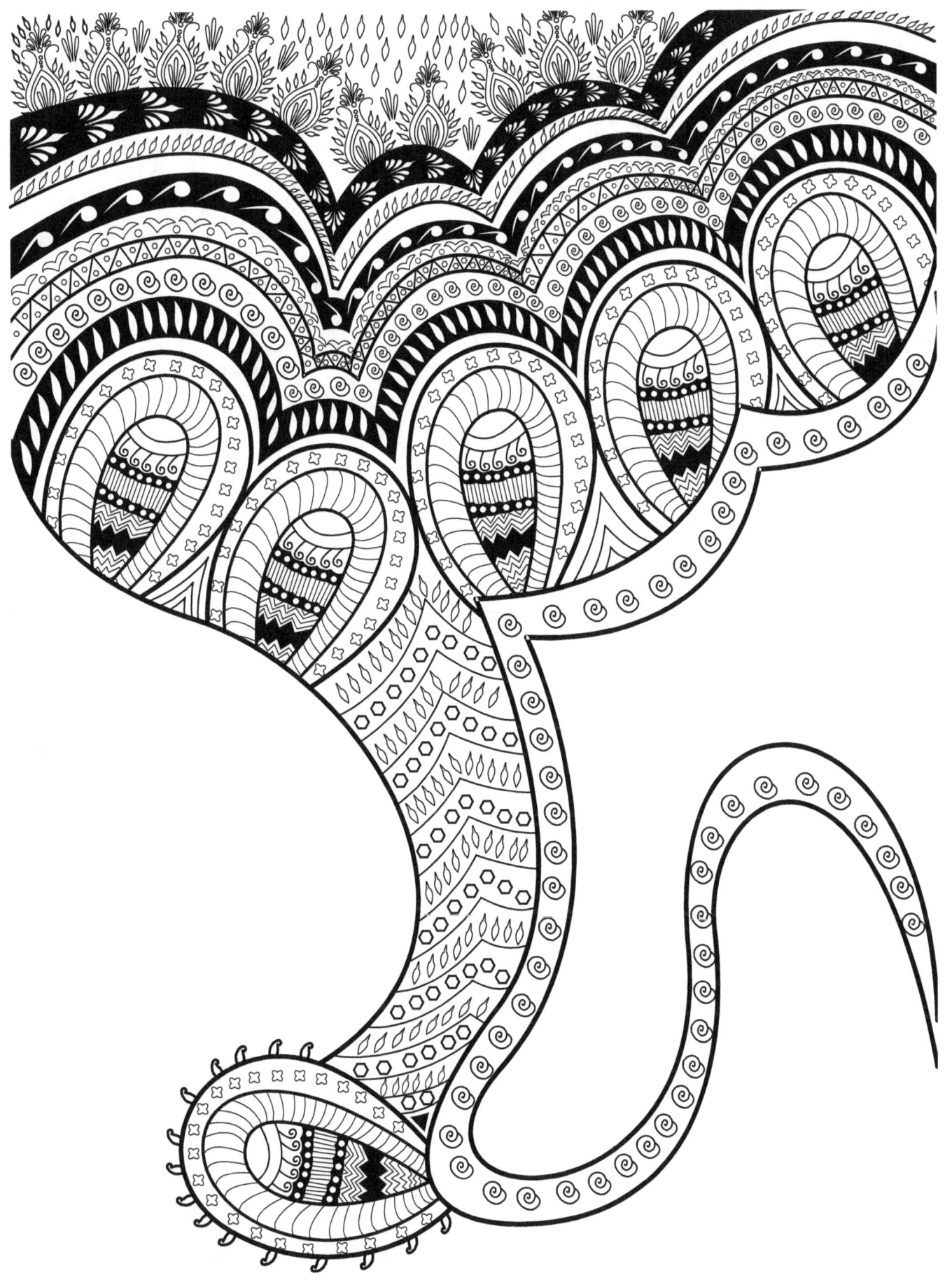

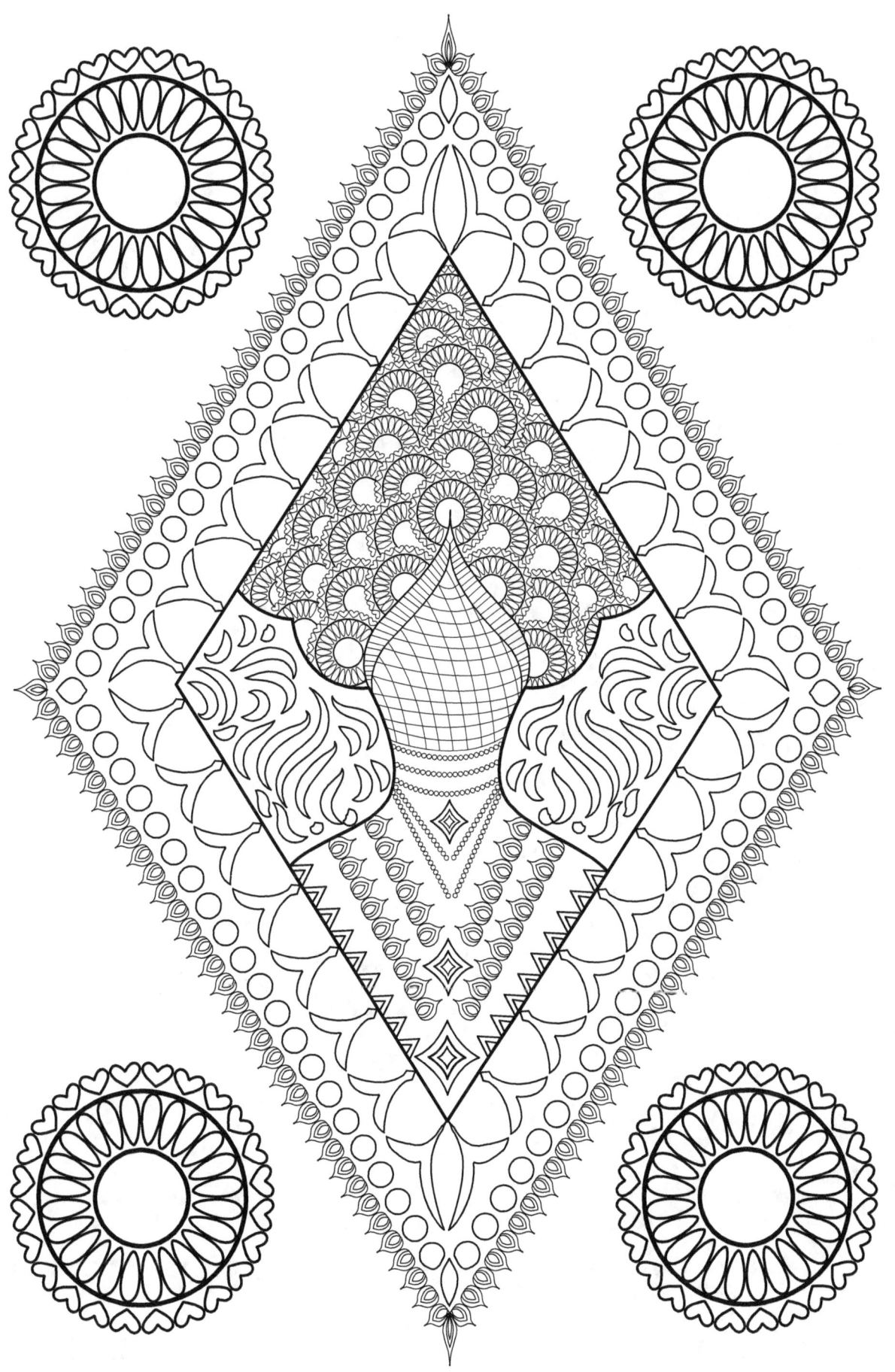

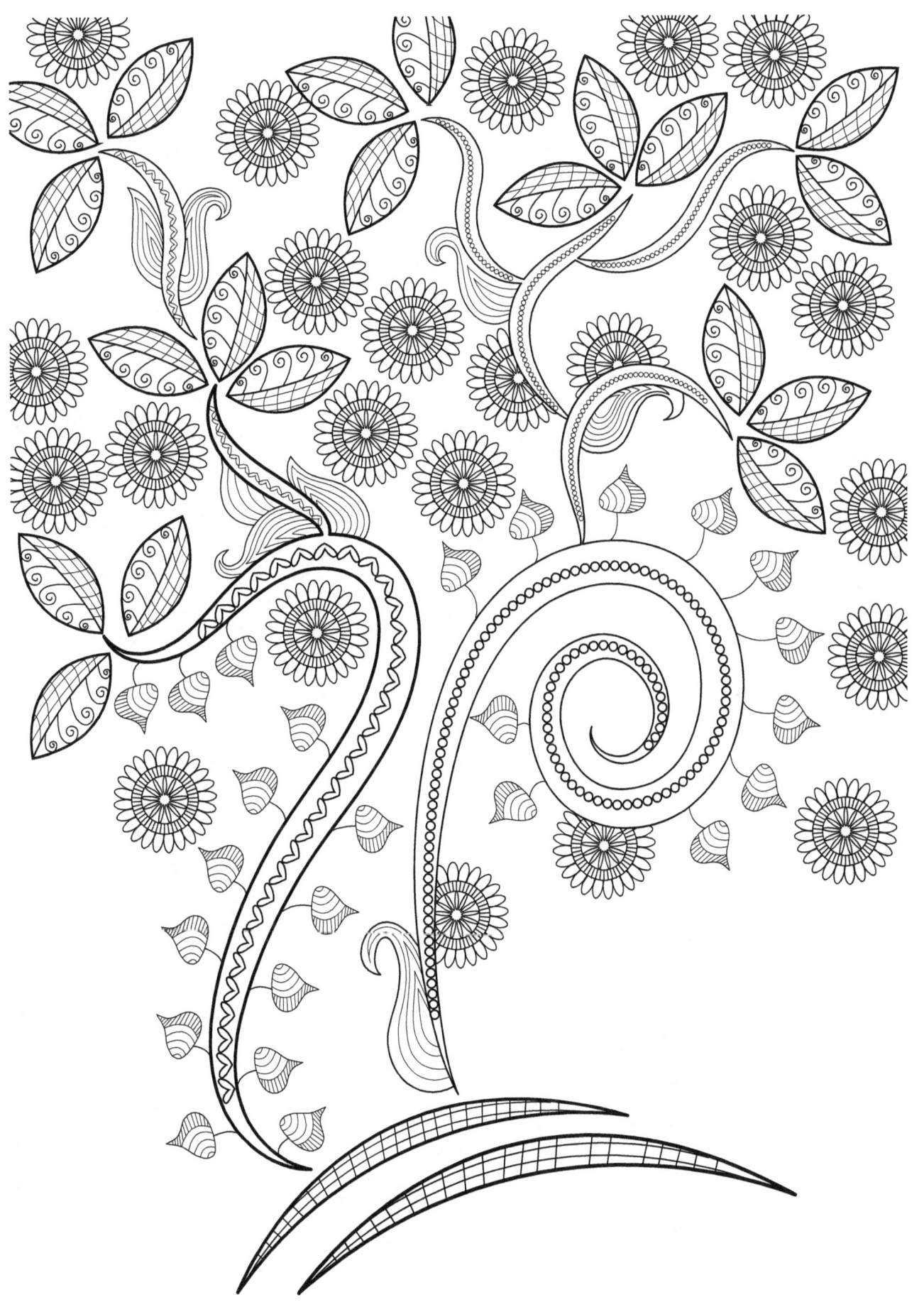

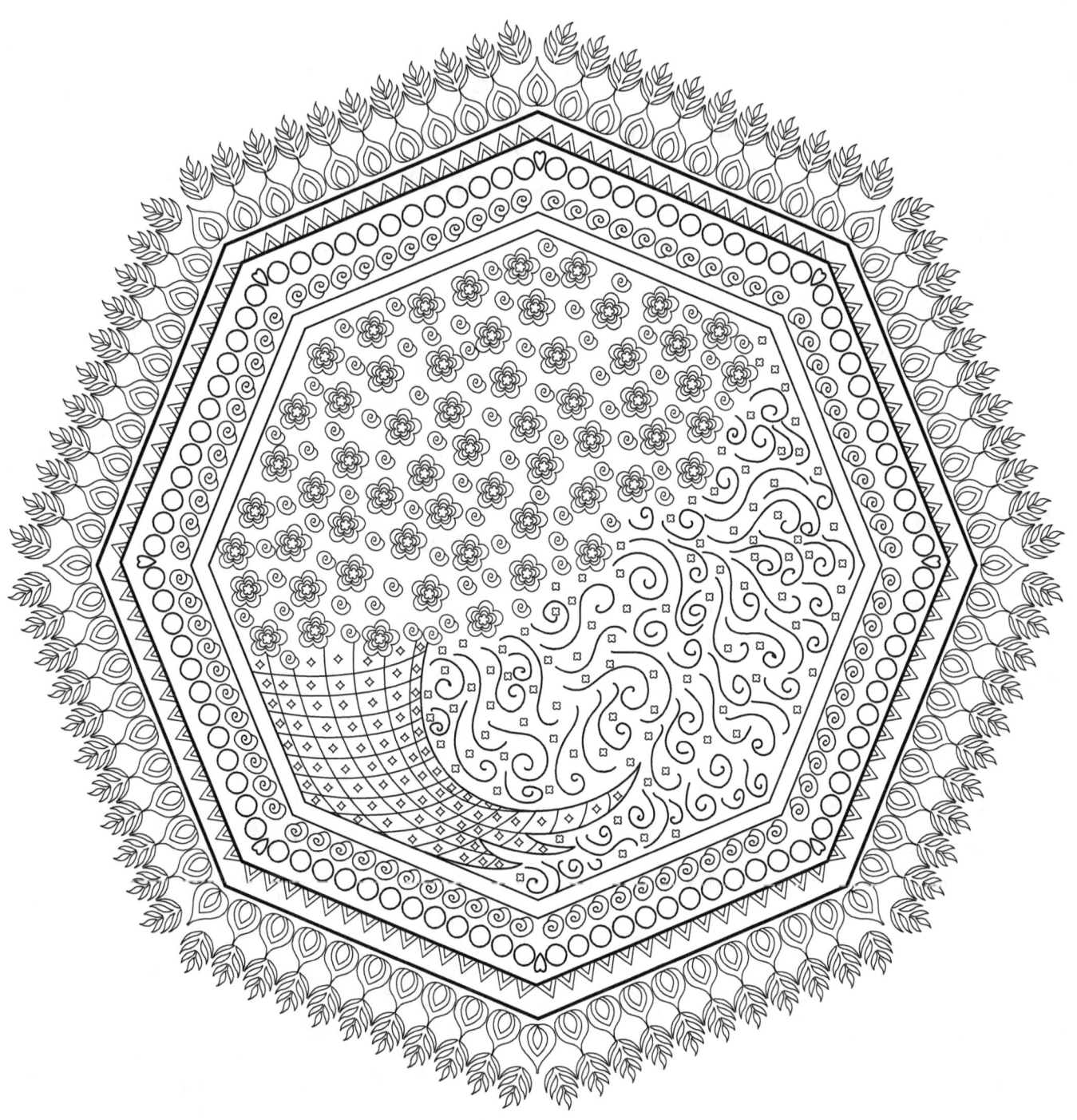

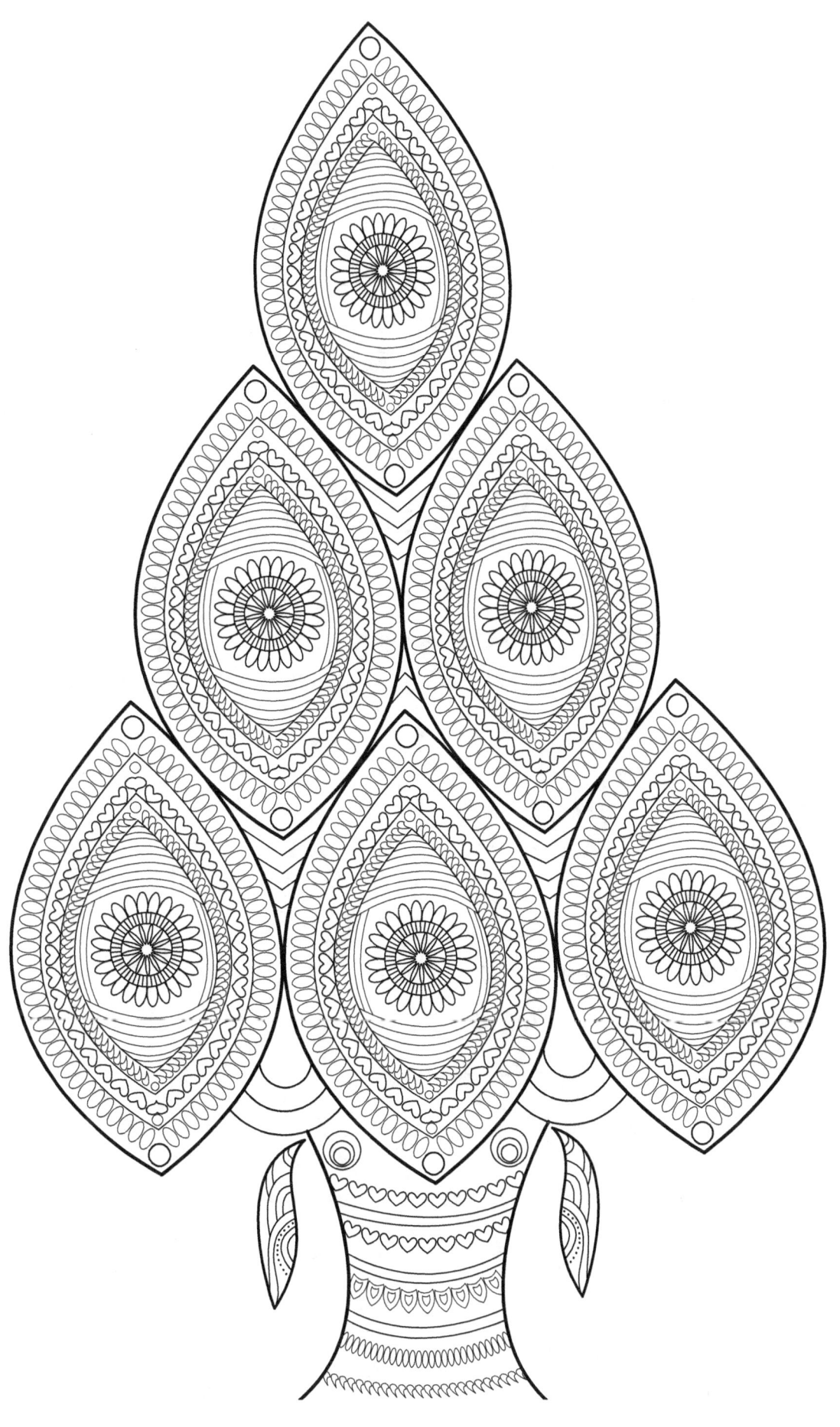

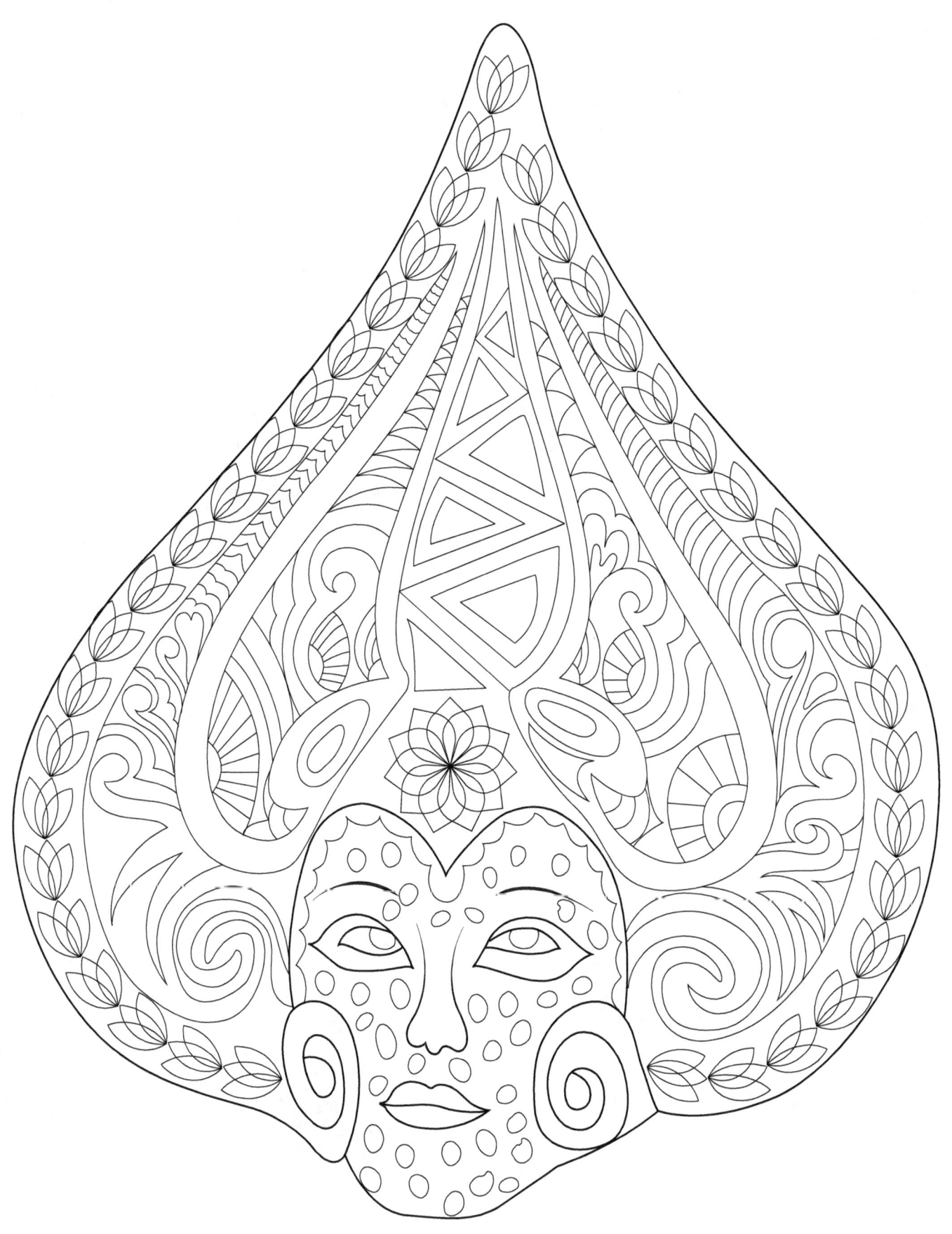

www.ingramcontent.com/pod-product-compliance
Lightning Source LLC
Chambersburg PA
CBHW080512220526
45465CB00006B/2461